SUCCESSFUL
SHOWING

Dedication

To the many friends I have made in the
showing world.

SUCCESSFUL SHOWING

Stuart Hollings

The Crowood Press

First published in 1991 by
The Crowood Press Ltd
Gipsy Lane, Swindon
Wiltshire, SN2 6DQ

British Library Cataloguing in Publication Data

Hollings, Stuart
Successful Showing.
   1.   Livestock. Horses. Showing
   I.   Title
   636.10888

ISBN 1 85223 271 4

Line-drawings by Sally Coles

Typeset by Alacrity Phototypesetters, Banwell Castle,
Weston-super-Mare

Printed and bound in Great Britain by BPCC Hazell Books Ltd, Aylesbury

Contents

Acknowledgements

The author wishes to express his grateful thanks to the following people for their invaluable help: Tom Best, David Blair, Jennifer Brown, Sandra Bucknell, Jill Caudle, Sally Coles, Dennis Colton, Peggy Grayson, Jerome Harforth, Stella Harries, Ben Harwood, Michael Hendrie, George Hollings, Nigel Hollings, Penny Hollings, John Keen, Victoria Keen, Anne Loriston-Clarke, Valerie Mallender, Ronnie Marmont, Robert Oliver, Donald Owen, Richard Ramsay, Madge Taylor, Richard Tomkinson, Vin Toulson, Joy Toynton, and to the photographers whose work appears in this book.

Introduction

There are many disciplines within the equestrian world which has witnessed a rapid development over the last twenty years. One of the most popular is showing, which has a very important role to play because the animals exhibited reflect the standard of the horse breeding industry and the show ring is a place that gives both horses and riders a good basic education in a varied competitive environment, at all levels, before moving on to other spheres. Jennie Loriston-Clarke, and her sister Jane Holderness-Roddam, Ted Edgar, Jamie Osborne, Peter Scudamore, Judy Bradwell and Jane Thelwall, all showed ponies as children before achieving success in their respective fields.

Fig 1   Norwood White demonstrating a novel way to attract the attention of his pony brood-mare Pendley Birthday Girl.

1 Native Breeds

The British Isles are unique in that they have no less than nine native pony breeds that are truly indigenous, not only to this country, but to the particular county or area from which they originate. All are very different in appearance (or type) having developed according to the habitat and job of work required of them, but all have the common characteristics of hardiness, sure-footedness, intelligence and the ability to survive on the poorest keep.

The British native pony will accomplish most jobs required of him but, of course, each breed may be better equipped physically or mentally for performing one particular job than for another.

The immense influence of our ancient and unique breeds, through the centuries right up until the present time, cannot be overestimated. Held in high esteem throughout the world, they are a valuable legacy to be treasured and preserved.

The Welsh Breeds

The Welsh ponies and cobs are now divided into four sections of which the smallest and probably best known is the Section A, the Welsh Mountain pony.

Section A The Welsh Mountain

The Welsh Mountain has a tiny head and ears, large lustrous eyes, deep compact frame, and the spectacular action that is the prerogative of all the Welsh breeds.

He does not exceed 12.0hh and, despite being the most glamorous of all native breeds, is also one of the most hardy: he has roamed the inhospitable mountainsides, picking a meagre living for centuries. His survival in such conditions lay in the fact that he was superbly proportioned to cope with the terrain and its environment and he could nourish himself on miniscule amounts of tough herbage. Today, life on the mountains, though still rigorous, is carefully supervised and controlled by the owners and in some measure by the Welsh Pony and Cob Society.

At one time, Arab blood was introduced into the breed; this had little far reaching effect on the breed as a whole, although the Arab outlook can still be seen in the wide cheeked head, delicate nostrils and fine dark eyes. Careful breeding has ensured a steady stream of beautiful animals to grace the show rings of the world. Some stallions have had a profound effect on the breed. One such was Dyoll Starlight, foaled in 1894; only by chance did this dominant sire come into being. His dam Moonlight, a flea-bitten grey, was born on the borders of Brecon and after passing through several hands came into the possession of the pony breeder Meuric Lloyd who used her as a driving pony for his wife. However, after being frightened in an accident involving dogs, Moonlight became a brood-mare and bred foals up to her thirteenth year. Her first, and most famous son, Starlight, was the result of a chance relationship

8

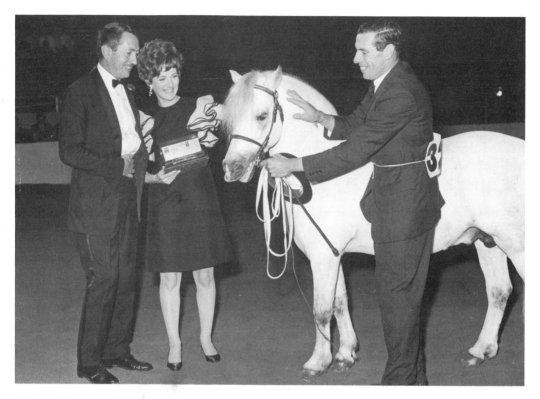

Fig 2   Treharne Tomboy, winner of the Fredericks In Hand Championship in 1968 and 1969, collecting his trophy from actress Barbara Murray who is accompanied by Fredericks Chairman Peter Sanders.

with a two-year-old colt. Starlight had a meteoric career in the show ring, seldom being beaten, and winning the Championship at the Royal Show at the age of twenty. Almost all today's grey Welsh Mountain ponies have him in their ancestry.

The Welsh Mountain pony is ideal for the ambitious child: he is beautiful, hardy, intelligent; and so constructed to produce fleet-footedness that he is capable of jumping either coloured or natural obstacles in fine style. The Section A may be any colour except piebald or skewbald.

Section B The Welsh Riding Pony

The Welsh Riding pony or Section B is the newest section in the stud book and grew out of a need for a bigger, quality riding pony for young people that could take his place alongside his thoroughbred brothers in the show ring. The Welsh riding pony was originally arrived at by crossing the Welsh Mountain with the small cob. However, in 1939, such was the demand for quality riding ponies for children that over the next decade or so, the Section B was upgraded by selective breeding to produce the elegance and

9

quality we find today. Not only does the Section B take his place in the show pony and working hunter pony rings with enormous success, he has also proved invaluable to cross with the thoroughbred to produce the highest quality riding ponies, for which high prices are paid by buyers, not only in this country but all over the world.

The basic Welsh structure remains the same: the good legs and feet and the characteristic head and eye, the good angle to the jaw and the big shoulder and length of rein. The body has perhaps taken on a more hunter-like appearance but the Section B is essentially a Welshman, both in appearance and hardiness,

and in his gay, bright Welsh spirit. Standing from 12.0hh to 13.2hh, he is in constant demand for the ring and as a hunter; elegant under saddle, and eye-catching between the shafts of a smart equippage, his intelligence and fleetness of foot enable him to carry riders successfully through the mounted games.

Sections C and D Welsh Cobs

The Welsh Cobs from the valleys of North and South Wales have been renowned for centuries for their handsome appearance, strength, quality and spectacular movement. Over the years, Welsh poets have been moved to write sonnets

Fig 3   Twyford Signal, a prolific winning Welsh Section B stallion.

*Fig 4   Turkdean Cerdin, Welsh Section C cob ridden here by
Pat Woods.*

in praise of the Welsh Cob, and in the sixteenth century Tudor Aled wrote this description which is as true today as when it was first written:

> The stallion should have the outlook and poise of a stag; the nostrils wide and open as the muzzle of a gun; the eyes, like two ripe pears bulging and dancing in the head; the ears, small and fine and restless like two sage leaves; the coat like new silk.

The breeding and training of Welsh Cobs has been carried on in the valleys by generations of people, many old families boasting of the years their ancestors were connected with this revered and peerless animal. It is less a breeding programme; more a religion. This breed is probably the most versatile of all the natives and some of the old stud cards of the last

century bear this out saying: 'Strong enough to work on the farm, swift enough to fetch the doctor in an emergency, hardy enough to put to the cannon, and good enough for the cavalry.' Always superb trotters, cobs found their way to the large cities in vast numbers, to draw trams and waggons, vans and carts, smart gigs and coaches. Trotting matches between these superb creatures meant fortunes were wagered and lost and won on the turn of a hoof. Men were justly proud of the appearance and performance of their cobs.

Today the cobs are divided into two sections: Section C, the Welsh pony of cob type not exceeding 13.2hh, a superb ride and drive animal, up to weight and ideal as a mount to bridge the gap for young people between pony and the

11

Fig 5   Llanarth Flying Comet, Welsh Section D cob, winner of the Lloyds final at Wembley in 1979 and 1980.

horse; and the Section D for which there is no height limit except in National Pony Society (NPS) national competitions where the limit is 14.2hh. Competing on equal terms with horses in ridden, jumping and cross-country events, the Section D has secured Royal patronage as Prince Phillip drives a team of four in competition. Crossed with the Thoroughbred to breed superb animals for eventing and show jumping, the Cob has devoted admirers and owners all over the world, and the best change hands at very high prices.

The basic overall shape of the Welsh Cob is the same as the Welsh Mountain's:

the small head with the wide angle to the jaw, the restless ears, wide-spaced, large intelligent eye, the deep strong body, big quarters and the magnificent legs and feet and, above all, the breath-taking movement with the great leverage from the rear and the whole of the shoulder and foreleg in use. A ring full of Cobs in action at a Welsh show is a sight not to be missed and never to be forgotten.

The affairs of the Welsh breeds are administered by the Welsh Pony & Cob Society, whose work and influence extends far beyond these shores, and whose care and diligence over the years has resulted in the four magnificent Welsh sections you see today.

The Irish Breed

Connemara

The Connemara is the only pony native to the whole of Ireland. Hailing from a wild, lonely region from Lough Corrib and Mask to the Atlantic and Galway Bay, this is a hardy pony with remarkably strong legs and feet. In the Middle Ages, Andalusian and Arab blood was introduced to improve looks and performance, and the breed found its way to England where, known as the Irish Hobby, he was in much demand as a pretty mount for ladies. (No doubt this is what our wooden 'hobby horse' is named after.) Today, he is found in ever increas-

Fig 6 Champion Connemara Leam Bobby Finn owned by Mr and Mrs J. Meade.

13

ing numbers in the show rings of the world.

The history of this pony is fairly well documented and in 1565, Blunville spoke of him as 'a pretty, fine horse, having a good head and being a pleasant ambler, but also useful for men with darts and spears.' Miss Pat Lyne, an authority on the breed, has collated all this history into a fascinating book entitled *Shrouded in the Mist*, which charts the pony's progress down through the ages to its more recent past as the peasants' and small farmers' work-horse and as a racing pony in country districts. Before roads were made, the Connemara hauled peat in panniers or on travois; then, as roads were built, in carts.

When living in their natural environment, the ponies grazing in the valleys have fairly lush grass but have to survive torrential rain and heavy gales. Those living in the hills have scant, scrub pasture, and nibble the gorse shoots, as does the New Forest pony; both breeds grow a 'gorse moustache' (a thick bush of hair to protect the delicate upper lip from the thorns).

Connemara affairs were administered from Ireland until 1947 when the English Connemara Society was formed, and this very active Society has done prodigious work in bringing the Connemara to the forefront of the native breeds. The height ranges from 13.0hh to 14.2hh and the breed has much the same lines as a small hunter, only with a pony head, large, kind eye, and well-shaped ear. Strongly limbed, they excel in the hunting field and in all sports across rough terrain, and are safe and admirable jumpers. In all performance competitions, they are successful right up to national level. The true, free action of the Connemara en-

sures a safe and comfortable ride. Many of the breed are grey, dun, bay or brown, but blacks and chestnuts do occur occasionally.

The English Breeds

Dartmoor

Today, only a very small percentage of the ponies seen roaming on Dartmoor are in fact true Dartmoor ponies. The large majority of the breed are in studs, many of which are situated in and around Dartmoor so that the breed has the benefit of his natural habitat with the added bonus of better feeding and housing. The first mention of ponies on Dartmoor comes in 1012 in the reign of the Saxon Bishop Aelfwold, and two centuries later it is recorded that the cost of grazing a pony on Dartmoor was two pence per year. Since the Middle Ages, little has been written about the Dartmoor pony, and it is not until the heyday of the tin mining industry that records show how much the tin miners relied on the native breed to transport tin to the Stannard towns. When the mines were worked out, the ponies were turned loose on the moor to fend for themselves, a few being sold to small farms for work as plough or draft animals, whilst some were crossed with Shetland stallions to produce a specialized pony for work in mines and pits. The Dartmoor pony is very strong for his size and, at one time, those measuring no more than 11.2hh carried their adult owners, regardless of weight, up and down the precipitous moorland about daily jobs on farms or holdings.

Up until as late as 1966, the prison Wardens at H.M. Prison, rode Dartmoor

Fig 7   Hisley Pedlar, supreme Champion Dartmoor at the
Royal Show four years in succession.

ponies when accompanying parties of prisoners who worked on the Moor breaking stone.

In 1898 the Polo Pony Society, later to become the National Pony Society, passed a resolution to issue a description of all the native breeds. The standard then issued for the Dartmoor pony differs little to that used for the breed today, except in the matter of height: in the latter half of the last century, stallions could measure 14.0hh and mares 13.2hh; now the breed does not exceed 12.2hh. As with many native breeds, Arab, Thoroughbred and Hackney blood have at various times been used to improve looks and performance.

The First World War was hard on the Dartmoor pony, as the Second was to be on the Exmoor. Many were taken for meat, and numbers were further decimated by the use of the Moor for Army training. In the 1920s, it was found necessary to pass a stallion, who had been sired by a desert bred Arabian. This stallion, called The Leat, had a great deal to do with the survival of the breed, and through his three daughters Juliet IV, Water Wagtail and Sparklet II, all today's animals trace back to him.

No doubt because of his good looks, quality and charming nature, the Dartmoor pony has, over the past sixty years, attracted many faithful admirers. In

15

appearance, he resembles a hunter in miniature, with small neat head, intelligent eye and small flexible ear, well-constructed, deep body, with a good length of rein, and the strong legs of the true native, with a well-shaped foot of hard horn. Couple all this with the free-flowing action, the natural jumping ability and the equable temperament, he makes a pony for anyone to be proud of. Crossed with the Thoroughbred pony, the Dartmoor breed has provided many of the most notable children's riding ponies to grace the rings over several decades. Well served by several active clubs, the parent Club is the Dartmoor Pony Society which caters for every sphere in which the breed is active.

Exmoor

Of the two native breeds of pony hailing from the west of England, the Exmoor is reckoned to be the oldest. Many theories have been propounded as to how he arrived on these shores, and the findings make fascinating material for discussion. Possibly the easiest to recognize of all the breeds, he is always bay or brown with distinctive mealy shading round the eyes, nostrils and under the belly. This breed is recorded in the Domesday Book as running on Lynton and Brendon. When Exmoor ceased to be a Royal Forest in the last century, Sir Richard Ackland drove 400 of the Exmoor ponies to his estates at Winsford Hill. In 1927, Mr. Frank Green took a share in the herd, and this share and Sir Richard's have now passed to the present owner Mrs. Wallace, making the famous Anchor Herd one of the most prestigious of all the Exmoor herds.

The First World War did little to affect the ponies on their native heath, but the Second World War nearly brought about its eclipse. Trigger-happy soldiers used the ponies as moving targets and decimated the hill regions. Whole areas of grass were rendered useless for grazing by tank training, and then large numbers of ponies were rounded up to be carted off and used for meat. It is only because the farmers on Exmoor managed to hide away some pure-bred stock, that the breed exists today but, even now it still figures on the Rare Breeds list.

Stallions measure up to 12.3hh, mares to 12.2hh, and the breed is superbly equipped to withstand the rigours of the Exmoor winters. A notable feature is the pony's weatherproof covering of dense soft coat, overlaid by long, fine greasy hair, which allows the water to run off and prevents snow from lying on the pony's back. The dock of the Exmoor fits snugly between the buttocks, while the hair at the root grows in a fan shape and acts as a snow chute. The head between the eyes is broad, and the bony ridge jutting above the eyes (known as the toad eye) acts as a protection from the icy particles of frozen rain. A heavy forelock, mane and tail further protects the animal from the elements. Ears are short, thick and well furred, nostrils large and well formed to enable the pony to inhale and exhale the freezing air when at a gallop. With his sturdy body, short, strong, well-boned legs with well-shaped open feet, the Exmoor is built to gallop on the uneven terrain of his native heath and is frequently used as a cross to the Thoroughbred or hunter mare to produce larger animals for hunting and riding on Exmoor and elsewhere. Now much sought after for all forms of equestrian activity, the Exmoor excels in rough

Fig 8   Dunkery Buzzard, Champion Exmoor, exhibited
by Miss J. Webb, in the East of England main ring.

country, and has also proved himself one of the most reliable breeds to work with the disabled. The Exmoor Pony Society, started in 1921, looks after the breed which, it is hoped, will soon be able to drop the frightening appellation of 'rare'.

New Forest

The New Forest pony roams an area which once stretched from the sea to the foot of the Wiltshire Downs. However, urbanization, the building of new roads and motorways, together with the enclosing (in the past twenty years) of many acres for camp sites, caravan parks, and car parks, as well as the fencing of the Forest, has greatly reduced the land available for the animals to graze. The New Forest was laid out as a royal hunting ground by William the Conqueror and

ponies have always grazed there. At one time, forming a source of revenue for the Crown, their affairs were administered by a warden. A court of verderers who sit at Lyndhurst several times a year, control the stallions in the Forest but have no control over the breed generally. Four agisters are appointed to safeguard the well being of the ponies; they patrol the Forest on horseback or, these days, more often in Land Rovers linked to each other by radio so that help can be obtained with great speed for any animal in trouble.

Over the centuries, people living in the Forest and deriving their livelihood from farming, woodcutting or heather cutting, used the ponies for transport and riding. In 1852, Queen Victoria sent her Arab stallion Zorah to the verderers for him to be turned out amongst the Forest mares

Fig 9 Willoway Pipers Gold, Champion New Forest pony showing his paces.

to improve the breed. Late in the century, a whole hotch-potch of breeds were turned out in a misguided attempt to better the breed. Welsh and Dartmoor, Exmoor and Highland, Fells and Arabs, and even a Basuto pony! Sir Berkeley Piggot, one of the great authorities on the New Forest pony, once wrote that 'owing to the mysterious ways of nature, all these breeds appear to have been ground down into one recognizable type known as the New Forest pony'. In 1891, an association for the improvement of the breed was set up and the New Forest Pony and Cattle Breeding Society, that today administers its affairs, came into being in 1906 as the Burley & District New Forest Pony Society.

As an all-round pony, the New Forest has few equals. He has the widest height range of all the natives and can be found as small as 11.2hh, to make the perfect leading-rein pony for the tiny child, up to 14.2hh, where he makes an admirable cross-country and hunting pony for a young person and adult. An accomplished performer in the show ring and at dressage, he also takes well to the shafts. With his equable temperament, he breaks easily and schools on intelligently. He has a pony head with no trace of horsiness and yet no dish of the Arab, clean lines, with a good length of rein, strong inback and quarters and a well-laid shoulder, strong limbs and good open feet. All colours are permitted except piebald, skewbald and blue-eyed cream.

The Fell and The Dales

The North of England boasts two ancient breeds: the Fell and the Dales. The Fell, the smaller of the two (not exceeding 14.0hh) comes from west of the Pennines, while the Dales at 14.2hh comes from the east. Until 1916, these ponies were considered different types of one breed. Since then, they have been separated into two distinct breeds, each with its own stud register. Both are descended from the Galloway pony of the Borders of Scotland, and one romantic tale is of black stallions, brought from Rome by soldiers manning Hadrian's Wall, intermingling with the native mares, their foals being ancestors of to-day's animals. Originally pack animals, both breeds are noted for their long, smooth stride at walk. As better roads were constructed, fast trotters were required and the Fell and Dales ponies were

crossed with the Norfolk roadster, producing such fast spectacular movers that they were greatly sought after in town and country and also used in trotting races. Signs of the old racecourses can still be seen in the north, and are marked on local maps.

Fell The Fell pony from the west side of the Pennines developed along the same lines as the Dales, principally as a pack animal carrying ore from east to west. But he was most used for carrying wool and cloth; as many as three hundred ponies a week passed through Kendal carrying wool. Trains of twenty animals, led by a mare with a bell fastened round her neck to warn other road users of their approach, carried the cloth the whole length of England to the ports, and returned laden with spices, canvas and oranges among their cargo. They would also carry butter and fodder, and it was

Fig 10   Barmston Queen, Champion Dale at the Great Yorkshire Show 1987.

Fig 11   Townend Richard IV, Champion Fell at the Ponies UK Stallion Show 1985 held on Brampton racecourse.

not unknown for them to carry contra-band! Farmers' wives drove them to market in small carts, or rode them while carrying baskets of eggs and butter to the nearest town, their equable temperament and long sure stride making them ideal for such work. A general work animal on the farms and holdings of the district, they were also ridden by farmers and shepherds tending flocks on the hills. Once the trotting breed had been introduced into them, Fell ponies, like the Dales, found their way in large numbers to the cities for use by tradesmen wanting swift animals to draw light turnouts for delivery work.

The Fell has a pony-like head with a bright eye, well-placed ears, a long clean neck to give a good length of rein to the rider, strongly bodied, with good quarters and limbs, and remarkable muscularity of thigh and forearm. One of the strongest boned of all the natives, they measure $8\frac{1}{2}$ inches (21.5 cm) below the knee. With his proud carriage, distinctive ground-covering movement and his flowing mane and tail, the Fell is now a popular competitive pony, highly successful in whatever sphere he finds himself. Well mannered and kind, he is suitable for even the most nervous rider, but

20

can prove to be an excellent jumper for the more ambitious. The Fell Pony Society formed in 1919 administers the affairs of the breed.

Dales   The Dales ponies, east of the Pennines, were largely used as pack animals to transport lead ore from the mines to the washing places and thence to ports on the coast, which involved distances of between thirty-five and forty miles. The ponies worked in gangs of twenty, loose headed and in the charge of one mounted man. As each animal carried two hundred-weight of ore, two tons were shifted in one journey. Dales were the work-horses of the farms and holdings, doing all the work on the land and, when roads improved, drawing wagon loads of fodder, timber and produce.

During the First World War, the Army bought up large numbers of the breed for use on the battlefields and in 1923, bought a draft of two hundred; all of these were over five years old, not exceeding 14.2hh with a girth of 68 inches (173 cm), weighing not less than half a ton and able to carry twenty-one stone over the mountains! Earlier in the century, many of the breed found their way to cities for use as vanners. World War Two saw the breed wanted only for meat, and over one thousand were taken to be slaughtered. In 1955, only four Dales mares were registered, and it is largely through a handful of Dalesmen searching out and finding others for inclusion in the Stud Register that the breed survived. It has been a long hard struggle but the dedication of the Dales supporters has achieved something of a miracle, even though today, demand for the Dales for riding and driving still outstrips supply.

Apart from his great strength and comparatively small compass, the Dales pony has a fine, handsome head, good length of rein and is noted for his strong legs and particularly his feet. On examining stallions in 1916, an inspector for the Board of Agriculture premiums remarked: 'The breed has one superb asset: the most perfect feet in the British Isles'. Today, the Dales appears in show rings around the country and riding, jumping and driving classes cater for him. The affairs of the breed are administered by the Dales Pony Society, who are fortunate to have at their head many senior Dalesmen who have known their breed over a long period.

The Scottish Breeds

Highland

The Highland pony has been bred on the mainland and the islands for many centuries and its history over the past eight hundred years is reasonably well documented. At one time there were two types of pony: the larger, heavier mainland type; and the smaller, lighter pony of the Western Isles. Mull Annan, Harris and Lewis, Erriskay, Tiree and Rhum all boasted their own particular type of Highland pony. All have now died out, although in recent years there has been an attempt to revive the local breed on Erriskay. Ponies from Rhum were at one time bought and turned out in the New Forest, and their distinctive hazel eyes can still be seen in their descendants. In the past, the Highland breed was used for all forms of work on farms and holdings and as a pack animal and, when roads improved, to draw all manner of private and commercial vehicles. They were used by shepherds and farmers as riding animals and, in the past as well as today, by sportsmen stalking deer; they ride the ponies up to the stalking grounds and then use them to transport the heavy stags down to the valleys. The famous Victorian artist, Landseer, immortalized the Highland pony in many of his best-known works depicting the Scottish country scene.

The Standard calls for a well-carried head, a moderate neck with clean throat, well laid back shoulders with a prominent wither, compact body with a natural curve, a deep chest and powerful hind-quarters, the whole supported on strong-ly boned legs and large open feet. From 13.2hh to 14.2hh, the Highland comes in a variety of pleasing colours as well as the familiar brown, bay and grey; the shades of dun, fox, mink and cream, gold, mouse, all with a dark eel stripe down the spine, are particularly attractive. A kind biddable breed that breaks easily and makes comfortable riding animals, the modern Highland pony takes part in all spheres of equestrian activity in the show rings and cross-country. His sure-footed-ness, intelligence and kindliness, together with his build and stamina make him an ideal mount for the growing family. The affairs of the breed are managed by the Highland Pony Society which encour-ages members in all forms of activity with their mounts.

Shetland

The history of the Shetland pony stretch-es back into the mists of time. One of the earliest pieces of evidence that the breed had inhabited the islands for some years came with the discovery on Burra Island of a stone carving of a monk with a very small pony; it was dated as ninth century. In the Middle Ages, the Shet-land was taken to the mainland of Scot-land for use as a pack animal, the country being so wild and rugged that larger animals were useless. At one time it was thought the Shetland was small because of the severe weather on the Isles and the small amount of stunted herbage avail-able for grazing, but when Shetlands were brought to the mainland and be-came widely distributed and bred from, they showed no increase in size and were then acknowledged as a true breed of small pony.

Despite their lack of size Shetlands are immensely strong and there is recorded a feat of one of the breed carrying a burden of two-and-a-half hundredweight across country for twenty-six miles. Used originally as pack animals and as trans-port for shepherds and farmers, they later pulled small carts and travois hauling wood, farm produce and crops. In the first half of the last century, drafts were sent for work in mines and many were crossed with Welsh and Dartmoor ponies to produce a small hardy breed to work in place of children after legislation for-bade the use of children in mines. Victor-ian American families discovered the Shetland and very large numbers of ponies were shipped to the States, mostly the light-coloured ones: piebald, skew-bald, chestnut, grey and cream, leaving the brown and black in the majority over here. Contemporary painting and early photographs in the States depict these colourful ponies in use as children's mounts and drawing little carts.

When adult, the height of the Shetland should not exceed 42 inches or 102 centimetres at the wither. He should

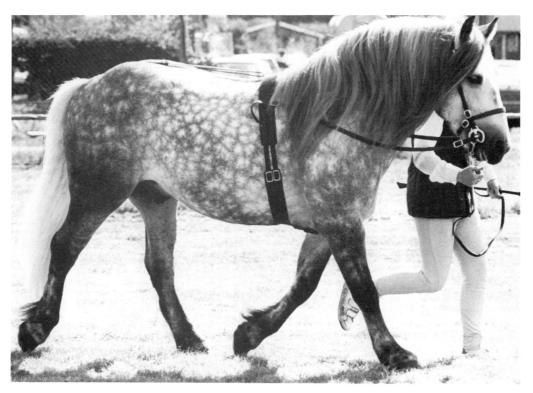

Fig 12   Dallas of Stanford, Highland Champion at the
National Pony Society Show 1987.

Fig 13   A Shetland Championship double for the Woods
family at Ponies UK Stafford Show with Champion Wells
Ernest (right) and Reserve Champion Lathom Jessica (left).

show quality without losing bone or sturdiness. He must have a small head with a large prominent eye, a strong shoulder and round rib (although not so round as to affect free movement). Quarters should be round and strong, and limbs must have sufficient flat bone with large, flat, fairly prominent knees. Strong open feet and straight, free movement is called for.

The Shetland Pony Stud Book Society is the oldest native pony society in the country and it is through their hard work that the breed is so popular today. An ideal first pony and friend for toddlers, the Shetland will also carry his young riders with ease into the hunting fields, and strongly contest all classes in the rings. The new Shetland Pony Grand National at Olympia has done much to bring the breed to the attention of the public.

2 Types

Judges must at all times consider the right type for the classes they are judging. In the pamphlet entitled 'Guidelines on Judging' issued by the British Show Hack, Cob and Riding Horse Association (BSHC&RHA), it says that one of the objects of the association is to improve the standard of hacks, cobs and riding horses, i.e. when judging a hack class it is important to place not the best entry, but the best hack entry.

Often horses do not win because they are entered in the wrong class and are therefore not the required type, even though they may have performed well in addition to having good conformation. In theory, a horse of true hunter type should not be able to win a hack class at a major show. In practice however, a horse of no definite type can sometimes be cleverly produced for a specific class.

The Hack

Originally, there were two types of hack: the covert hack and the park hack. Before the days of the horse-box, the covert hack would carry the hunting men and women to the meet, (amongst other duties) at a quicker pace covering more ground but still in comfort, before they changed over to their hunters which the groom had previously walked to the rendezvous.

The park hack is similar to today's show hack and was ridden by the fashionable ladies and gentlemen in the city parks, most notably in Rotten Row, which commanded a very strict code of etiquette. He should be an ornamental animal with style and elegance; perfect to look at and a delight to watch, with manners, presence, graceful extravagant action and above all intelligence, without which he would never be a pleasant ride. His head should be of the finest oriental type, the neck well-arched, the shoulders light at the points, long and grown well into the back. The loins should be accurately arched and quarters level and nicely rounded, not dropping abruptly toward the tail. The mane and tail should be straight without the least suspicion of a curl, every hair as soft as silk. Four clean, well-shaped, well-placed legs, the fetlocks rather longer than would be chosen for the hunter. From such a form, action which should be pleasant for the rider, may be confidently expected and paces agreeable even for the most ignorant observer to follow.

The walk should be fast and springy, the legs moving independently of the body. From this, he should be able to bound into any pace in perfectly balanced action. This, and the hand canter which you seldom see today, were the original paces of the park hack – galloping was not permitted in the park as speed was not of the essence and the trot was for the groom and usually associated with the covert hack. The object of riding in the park was to see and be seen and the hack was in modern-day terms the 'poseur's' horse. It was not uncommon for a hack to canter alongside another that was walking

Fig 14   Lady Teller, Hack of the Year 1968, 1969 and 1970 with her jockey David Tatlow who is wearing the correct park dress for final judging.

whilst the riders were held in polite conversation – the origin of the pairs class.

To perform the hack canter properly, the hack must be collected and brought almost to a standstill on his haunches. It is difficult to find a horse to canter pleasantly and slowly in a grand and graceful style because the strength required in the loins, hocks and thighs to perform such a pace throws so much strain on these muscles and tendons, and the combination of strength and soft action is rare. It was thought that no hack was worthy of the name if he would not, at the slightest indication, canter at the rate of 6mph. Some people attempt to perform this slow canter, usually in four-time, often with novice hacks who have not yet learnt to go forward, with the eventual result

that the horse will not respond when asked to open up by the judge. Also, so many hacks nowadays are too much on the forehand, something which is difficult to correct if, say, the horse is higher behind than in front but easy to avoid in one of good make and shape.

Whereas the covert hack was the introvert horse, the park hack was the extrovert of the two and would often need skilled riding. Sir Robert Peel was in fact killed when riding an unsuitable horse that shied. The late Lord Palmerston wrote to his brother in Naples after Peel's death: 'Peel was a very bad horseman and a very awkward rider — his horse might have been sat on by any better equestrian and he seemed somehow to have forced the horse to have stepped or knelt on him'. Just before Sir Robert Peel bought

*Fig 15   Ridgewood Venture, with Stella Harries, twice
Champion Hack at the RIHS and winner of the Winston
Churchill Cup at the same show in 1974, when their
performance was described as 'poetry in motion'. This large hack
never won at The Horse of the Year Show, 'as he was not a
"concrete" animal'.*

the horse that killed him, he refused to buy a perfect hack called The Premier (after a full trial) because he could not believe that anyone would give £400 for a hack.

There are few hacks being exhibited today which could be classed as the true type and it will be interesting to see how much influence the newly introduced hack breeding classes will have on improving the situation. Some experts think very little since we have lost the small Thoroughbred polo pony stallion that played such an important role. The ideal type is still the Thoroughbred – or one that looks and feels like it – full of quality with good limbs and movement and certainly not a weed. Even though there are some riding horse/covert hacks being exhibited in the large class (over 15hh – 15.3hh), some of the Champions from this section are of the correct type. Whereas, in the small class (14.2hh – 15hh) one does see a preponderance of pony types which are very attractive, often ridden by junior riders or young ladies weighing about seven stones, but which would not, one feels, be capable of carrying a mature

*Fig 16   Shalbourne Last Waltz, Small Hack of the Year 1970
and 1971. Originally shown as a large hack (coming second to
Ridgewood Venture at the Royal) she was the last horse Harry
Tatlow showed in top hat and tails when standing Reserve to
Prince of Wales ridden by son David (seen here) at the RIHS.*

adult for any distance or length of time. Ideally, the small hack should be up to more weight than the large hack and give a big ride. Even though the Thoroughbred horse carries from many generations back a trace of Arab in his blood, some of the exhibits in today's hack classes – particularly in the small class – exhibit more than a trace, which like the pony breeding is possibly the way to keep the height down.

If you are able to afford a Thoroughbred horse of the correct height out of training, you are often disappointed to find that his temperament has been spoilt and he will not do the job, because good manners are an important part of the hack's repertoire. Some producers feel that we are taking the manners consideration too far and expecting the impossible; a hack that has a look of the eagles yet does not even twitch an ear, lest he be considered unsuitable. As a result, many of the hacks look bored and mechanical, something which would not have attracted attention in Rotten Row. After all, as one top professional remarked, 'If my hack reacts to a tractor that backfires at the side of the ring, at least I know that he's not deaf or blind; and if there was a hole in the ring, I would rather my horse take exception to it than fall in!' The

*Fig 17   Brown Buzzard, Hack of the Year 1981 and 1982
(ridden here by Cathryn Cooper), half-brother to Dragonhill
Rushlight (Junior Jumper of the Year 1981).*

worst type of horse, according to John Keen, is the unpredictable one in the ring; 'the house angel but street devil!'

Apart from being a pleasure to ride, a well-schooled horse will excel in other spheres; Lucky Strike came from the race track and won the Hack of the Year in 1962 when trained by Count Robert Orssich and ridden by Annie Davey; and then went on to win the puissance competition at the Horse of the Year Show in the capable hands of Malcolm Pyrah. A hack called Brigand which I produced to become Reserve Champion at the White City and Birmingham Shows had been evented before becoming a show horse; and then was a successful small, light-weight and working hunter before being shown as a hack.

A top-class hack should also be a good and easy 'sit-on', being as light as a feather so that it can be ridden on the buckle or with one hand, whereas the riding horse can be ridden with more contact. The Champion hack should per-form an individual show fluently so that the transitions are easy and smooth, like those of a duck on water. On no account should anyone attempt to execute some-thing which is beyond the rider's or horse's capabilities and, if incorporating any dressage-type movements like a half pass or a flying change in a Champion-ship, these should be smooth, elegant and unexaggerated and not make the rider look busy or the horse look Germanic. Even though riders used to perform high-school movements in the park to attract the attention of their admirers, these are to be avoided in the show ring. If one bears in mind the history of the show hack, one can fully understand why presentation is probably more relevant in the hack class than in any other showing class and how an elegant rider, suitably mounted, can win a class on artistry alone.

29

*Fig 18   Right Royal, Hack of the Year 1971, 1972, 1973
and 1974 with four different jockeys: Vicky Spencer Cox
(in photo), Vera Holden, Marjorie Ramsay and Fiona O'Neil.*

*Fig 19   Tenterk,
Hack of the Year
1977, 1978 and
1979, with profes-
sional showman
Robert Oliver in the
saddle.*

Fig 20   Leamington Moon River, Hack of the Year 1975 and 1976, ridden by Jennie Loriston-Clarke.

Hack of the Year at The Horse of the Year Show from 1949

1949	Liberty Light	1969	Lady Teller
1950	Liberty Light	1970	Lady Teller
1951	Festival Maid	1971	Right Royal
1952	Honeysuckle	1972	Right Royal
1953	Lovely Boy	1973	Right Royal
1954	Gentle Lady	1974	Right Royal
1955	Replaced by riding horse classes but returned with two classes.	1975	Leamington Moon River
		1976	Leamington Moon River
1956	Regina	1977	Tenterk
1957	Sea Breeze	1978	Tenterk
1958	Kavora Another Star	1979	Tenterk
1959	Desert Storm	1980	Royal Return
1960	Juniper	1981	Brown Buzzard
1961	Desert Storm	1982	Brown Buzzard
1962	Lucky Strike	1983	Loch Lomond
1963	Mirage	1984	Fair Change
1964	Smooth Talk	1985	Ryetangle
1965	Berrydon Lad	1986	Ryetangle
1966	Feudal Knight	1987	Ryetangle
1967	Moonstrike	1988	Formidable
1968	Lady Teller	1989	Agar Heir Apparent

N.B. The show moved from Harringay to Wembley in 1959.

The Cob

For centuries, this all-rounder has been one of the glories of England. He is the John Bull of the equine world: stocky, powerful, of a round symmetrical form, without the speed or elasticity of the hunter nor the elegance of the hack, and yet ever willing and reliable with an individuality of his own.

The following definition of cobs and their history is based on a description by the late Douglas Mould who in his time was one of the leading hackney judges in the world. He died in 1979 aged ninety-three and his grandfather, William Bramley, was arguably the largest owner and hirer of riding horses and carriage horses in London.

Many years ago, the average man was considerably shorter than he is today; and men of the leisured classes were also likely to be overweight since most of their long social hours were spent consuming large, heavy meals and copious amounts of alcohol. Consequently, their horses could not be too large (otherwise the riders would look too small), and yet they had to be strong, easy to mount and of an extremely sober disposition. In order that a slightly dispepsic tummy or thick head would not be caused undue discomfort, its movement had to be soft and smooth: an easy walk at over 4mph, a square trot at 5mph and a perfect slow canter performed on the haunches. It also had to be a most attractive animal to the eye and of good colour (these gentlemen would never be seen on a washy or mealy horse), and so the cob required by these gentlemen was what is, today, a show cob. The requirements were quality, with a large, bold and generous eye, a well-bred intelligent head, a large front

Fig 21   Sport, six times Cob of the Year. Many judges described him as 'a very obedient ride'.

well set on at both ends (wither and jowl), a good, soft light mouth and 'manners to burn'. A good short forelimb with well-shaped feet, low, smooth action and a tremendous depth of girth combined with a wither designed for riding not driving. The quarters had to be strong and broad but again not losing quality with a good hind leg and a flowing tail high set. In those days, the tail would be docked; this practice became illegal in the 1950s. In short, the cob had to have the strength of the dray horse, the quality of a racehorse and the manners of a perfect gentleman.

These horses commanded an extremely high price equal to or greater than the best Leicestershire hunters because they were bred by chance and were expected

Fig 22 Just in Time, Cob of the Year 1974, discovered in Ireland in a trap taking milk to the creamery.

to be able to carry up to seventeen stones (108 kg). Some of these animals were also used as hunters and these had to be beautifully schooled as they were expected to be outstanding performers but never to be strong. A cob of proper sober colour was worth 200 guineas to a dealer in 1878 and when a heavyweight millionaire or timid seven-stone man came to him in despair the dealer could ask any price he wished.

The next type of cob could be compared to today's working cobs. They were used in the country by the doctor, the vicar and the better off yeoman farmer. These cobs worked during the week carrying the doctor on his rounds in the trap and the farmer to market. Sometimes they were used to convey the children to school, often riding one behind the other. On Sunday they would take the family to church in the trap, having attended the hunt for a few hours the day before. (They even had leather overshoes to wear when mowing the lawn.) They did not have to have the quality, beauty or presence of the London elitist cob, but for the regular work, had to be of good basic conformation and comfortable enough to be used for riding and driving.

This animal had to be reliable and

*Fig 23 Cromwell, Cob of the Year 1976, by Autumn Gold
(by Nearco) ex an I.D. Mare and bred by James Corbett of
Co. Clare. Originally sold for £60 at a fair, in his career he won
£4,200 in prize money, was Champion at the Royal three times
and Hickstead eleven times, apart from representing his RC at
national level and leading the Horseman's Parade in London
three times.*

trustworthy – he was a member of the family. Once bought as a four-year-old, say, he would remain with the family for the rest of his life. Therefore, soundness was also of paramount importance since he was likely to be the only animal the family had. In comparison to the show cob of the time, the working cob was worth between £50 and £100, could carry up to fourteen stones (89 kg) and move at a fair pace with useful but not showing action.

The third type of cob was the vanner which, unfortunately, are sometimes seen in the ring today. They were, however, the least valued type, used by the greengrocers, butchers and milkmen. Some of these tradesmen could afford a more flashy cob and so the occasional good Welsh Cob or Hackney cross could be found but, in the main, these animals were poor specimens, tied in at the knee and elbow with knee action and little importance was attached to faults such as dishing or plaiting. They were mean of the head and eye with poor fronts and straight shoulders, and no depth of girth (herring- and string-gutted). They usually had pinched quarters and a low-set tail. Having said this, these animals quite often worked unbelievably long hours on the most meagre and sparse rations and with very little care and attention so, often, only the fittest survived. The better of these animals were often sold by sharp dealers to ignorant people who had acquired enough money to aspire to a riding horse: the legs were carefully shaved, tails nicked to give them carriage and their coats prepared to the utmost. The buyer who knew no better viewed with great admiration the high action of the horse at a fast butcher-boy trot. However, in the main, they gave a very bad ride – the straight shoulders and high action making them unable to cover much ground in spite of exerting a great deal of energy. The wear on the joints due to poor conformation and being ridden hard on surfaces such as cobbles was marked and unsoundness would soon develop.

With the advent of the motor car, which set a seal on the life of the doctor's cob, a fourth cob emerged at the same time that polo in the Raj was starting. This is the type which is sometimes shown today in the lightweight classes: the small hunter/polo pony type, which was not to be confused with the quality, little, blood horse used by a very small man of more moderate means in the shires for hunting, or by a man who wished to have two of these horses for hunting rather than one large animal, which would cost the same to keep. It was not a common vanner but more of a riding animal with better action.

To bring the picture up to date, the show cob was the Rolls Royce, the doctor's cob the Vauxhall estate, and the vanner the delivery van.

Today's show cob is either shown as a lightweight (which should have at least 8½ inches (21.5 cm) of bone) or a heavyweight (which should have at least 9 inches (23 cm) of bone and be able to carry fourteen stones (89 kg) or over). Neither should exceed 15.1 hh, which has caused much debate over the last couple of seasons. The traditionalists wish to keep the height as it stands at present, feeling that the type may be lost if the height is increased to 15.2 hh, since we may then let in the cobby, small hunter with its bigger ride which would dominate the classes over the genuine cob type. Also, raising the height limit would set a precedent and the hack people may very well put forward a good argument for raising the heights of the hacks, saying quite convincingly that the small hack would be more of a little horse were it 15.1 hh; and many of the racehorse types, which up to now have been too big, would then become good large hacks if the limit were raised to 16 hh. Personally, I can see no harm in raising the cob heights to 15.2 hh in the working classes: this would set no precedent since we have no working hack and riding horse classes and at least the over-height cob would then have a showing class to compete in whereas, at the moment, the genuine cob over 15.1 hh is redundant.

The argument for raising the height to 15.2 hh lies in the fact that because many cobs are cold bred and are often of Irish Draught breeding (which is also the reason that some are back at the knee), they grow rapidly when fed and worked for the show ring. Consequently, many cob enthusiasts are paying vast sums for potential cob Champions, unbroken and untouched, only to find that there is a very strong risk of their growing over the permitted height before they fully mature.

Economical to keep and able to be ridden by all members of the family, young and old and of various shapes, the cob classes have experienced an incredible increase in popularity over the last several years and exhibitors can now compete at many levels in novice, working and amateur owner classes in addition to the two weight categories.

The late Count Robert Orssich used to carry a photograph in his wallet of Mrs Rosemary Cooke's outstanding cob Alexander who reigned supreme for four seasons in the 1950s. He was found in Ireland pulling a cart complete with mane on. Orssich bought the cob leaving the vendor with a problem, as he had to think of a way to take the cart, which was fully laden, back home!

Fig 24 *Just William, three times lightweight Cob of the Year owned by racehorse trainer John Dunlop, and ridden by Roy Trigg who said, 'He is outstanding because he always pulls out bright and is a super ride'.*

Cob of the Year at The Horse of the Year Show from 1949

1949	Knobby	1970	Johnathon
1950	Nutmeg	1971	Vodka
1951	George	1972	Johnathon
1952	Alexander	1973	Johnathon
1953	Badger	1974	Just in Time
1954	Tommy	1975	Grand View
1955		1976	Cromwell
1956		1977	Kempley
1857	No classes held	1978	Kempley
1958		1979	Kempley
1959		1980	Brock
1960	Bronze Boy	1981	Ducklys Huggy Bear
1961	Charlie	1982	Grandstand
1962	Sport	1983	Grandstand
1963	Sport	1984	Grandstand
1964	Sport	1985	The Irish R.M.
1965	Sport	1986	Grandstand
1966	Button	1987	Superted
1967	Sport	1988	Just William
1968	Sport	1989	Super Ted
1969	Johnathon		

Fig 25   Spey Cast (middleweight), Show Hunter of the Year 1965 with the late Jack Gittins aboard.

The Show Hunter

Compared to the hack, who must be graceful and elegant, the hunter must be powerfully built, properly proportioned in body and limbs, with plenty of stamina to gallop and last through a hard day's hunting, possess a bold heart to tackle various obstacles and have the sense and manners to carry out his task with merit. Although the show hunter is not required to prove himself in the hunting field, he should still be ideal in make and shape and, above all, he should be sound. Here follows a description of the hunter as seen in 1831:

The hunter is in value and beauty next to the racer ... he should seldom be under 15hh or more than 16hh. Below this standard, he cannot always sufficiently measure the object before him and above this he is apt to be leggy and awkward at his work ... As the agriculture of the county improves, the speed of the chase is increased ... the character of the hunter is consequently gradually changing. Stoutness is still required, but speed is becoming more necessary and, therefore, for the fox and the deer and even for the hare, blood is an essential quality. The first property of a good hunter is that he should be light in hand. For this purpose, his head must not be large ... but must be well set on. The hunter may be our companion and our servant through a long day and it is of essential consequence that he should not too much annoy and tire us by the weight of his head and neck. The forehand should be loftier than that of the racer ... and barrel should be rounder to give greater room for the heart and lungs to play ... similarly, a broad chest is an excellence in the hunter ... the majority of horses that perish in the field are narrow chested. The arm should be as muscular as that of the courser or even more so, for both strength and endurance are wanted and the legs should be broader than

that of the racehorse, especially beneath the knee. A racer may be tied in below the knee without perfectly destroying his power but a hunter with this defect will rarely have stoutness and the leg should be shorter. Higher action is required than in the racer, that the legs may be clearly and safely lifted over many an obstacle and particularly that they may be well doubled-up in the leap. The pastern should be shorter and less slanting yet retaining considerable obliquity. The hunter from his different action does not require the elastic mechanism of the long pastern; he more needs strength to support his own heavier carcase and the greater weight of his rider and to undergo the fatigue of a long day.

The foot of the hunter is the most impor-

Fig 26 Bunowen, by Seven Bells, Hunter of the Year in 1977 and 1978 when shown as a lightweight by David Tatlow, after which he became a middleweight when the weight category moved down from 13 to 12st 7lbs.

*Fig 27   Top Notch, Show Hunter of the Year 1969 and
1970, by Top Walk. A rare pattern of a middleweight
hunter.*

tant point. The work of the racer is all performed on the turf and his bad feet may scarcely incommode him, but the foot of the hunter is battered over many a flinty road and stony field and, if not particularly good, will soon be disabled and ruined. The body should be short and compact compared with that of the racehorse that he may not in his gallop take too extended a stride – this would be a serious disadvantage in a long day when going over clayey, poached ground during the winter months. The compact, short-strided horse will almost skim the surface, while the feet of the larger reached animal will sink deep and he will wear himself out by efforts to disengage himself. Every horseman knows how much more enduring is a short-bodied horse in climbing hills.

The rider needs not to be told how essential temper and courage are. A hot, irritable brute is a perfect nuisance and the coward that will scarcely face the slightest fences exposes his owner to ridicule.

Library of Useful Knowledge:
The Horse with a Treatise on Draught.

Hunter classes are normally divided into three weights (the weight of the rider and his saddle, which the animal is considered capable of carrying for a day's hunting: the lightweight, up to 12 stones 7 pounds (79.5kg); the middleweight, 12 stones 7 pounds to 14 stones (79.5–89kg); and the heavyweight, 14 stones (89kg) or over. Capacity is assessed not by height but

Fig 28 Seabrook, Show Hunter of the Year 1984, 1986 and 1987, under the spotlight after winning the Supreme Championship at the RIHS in 1986. Vin Toulson is wearing the correct dress for final judging.

by the amount of bone (measured by its circumference) below the knee and its quality. A little less Thoroughbred limb will have a greater density than more common bone and will therefore be up to more work. The ideal lightweight hunter should be around 16.1hh with around 8½ inches (21.5cm) of bone; the middle-weight about 16.3hh with 8¾–9 inches (22–23cm) of bone below the knee; and the heavyweight, 9–10 inches (23–25cm) of bone. If a judge decides a hunter is up to more weight, he can ask the horse to move up to the next class. The procedure for this is detailed in the rule book.

Unlike the hack or pony, the hunter is not asked to give an individual show so the rider must have the horse going well in front of the judge as he rarely has a second chance to show off the horse's paces, although I have once or twice seen two horses in close contention riding off against each other before the judge finally made his decision. When the judge rides, the horse must give him a comfortable but courageous ride, in other words, take the judge a little. The hunter's action must cover the ground more than the hack as his job is to carry a person across country and not take all day about it. A bad gallop is one in which the horse flies off the handle with his head in the air like a demon possessed or gallops into the ground, pounding up and down like a car with a flat tyre. The good galloper is one that lowers the head and neck and lengthens the stride, gliding along the grandstand like a car in overdrive. Judges may overlook a small fault if a hunter can gallop very impressively and pull up obediently without a fight.

Many Champion show hunters are retired from the show ring prematurely because they become very ringcrafty and particularly anticipate the gallop. Many top hunter exhibitors would like their horses to be asked to change the rein or be asked to do something different, possibly an individual show, to overcome this.

Although in theory, manners are extremely important in these classes, it would be true to say that these judges are not as strict as they are in hack or pony classes. The hunter judging panel includes many talented people from all circles, whether it be racing or eventing, who are quite capable of forgiving a minor *faux pas* if the hunter has given them a good ride, for example. This is often the reason that many good hunters are rarely beaten, even on an off day, and so the form book remains consistent. According to one top professional, good horses are difficult to find and no judge is going to admit that they cannot ride a big winner!

The lightweight class can contain a mixed bag of horses ranging from the lighter type of horse, which is also suc-

Fig 29   Burrough Hills, ridden by Jane Kent (now McHugh). Small Hunter of the Year 1957 to 1959, and Riding Horse of the Year 1955.

Small Hunter of the Year at The Horse of the Year Show from 1954	
1954 Rightaway	1972 Roulette
1955 Silver Streak	1973 Sporting Print
1956 Fonmon	1974 Smasher
1957 Burrough Hills	1975 Sporting Print
1958 Burrough Hills	1976 Footpath
1959 Burrough Hills	1977 Footpath
1960 Pelicamp	1978 Misty Day
1961 Tomboy	1979 Statesman
1962 Some Gardener	1980 Royal Gossip
1963 Pelicamp	1981 Sealord
1964 Savoya	1982 Highland Bound
1965 Some Gardener	1983 Statesman
1966 Some Gardener	1984 Little John
1967 Little Buzzard	1985 Macbeth
1968 May Queen	1986 Little John
1969 Newton Belle	1987 Little John
1970 Lord Sorcerer	1988 Swindon Wood
1971 Sportsman	1989 Small Print

cessful in a large riding-horse class, to one which is bordering on a middleweight. The latter is the type that has the advantage at the shows that hold only two weight classes. The ideal lightweight however is a blood horse with limb and substance who is a good mover, gives a very light accurate ride and gallops well without pulling. Many top lightweight horses have also competed with enormous success in ladies' classes which could be the reason that this type of horse is extremely popular and the lightweight classes are often the best filled at major shows. Another reason is that there does seem to be more lightweight horses in supply although it takes an outstanding one from this weight category to clinch a major Championship.

If one is to describe the lightweight as a good ladies' horse, the middleweight hunter could easily be defined as suitable for the average man and he is often the one which satisfies most judges' interpretation of the perfect Champion show hunter. Some Champions from this division that I particularly enjoyed watching were Top Notch, Elite and Dual Gold.

It must be everybody's dream to find and produce a quality heavyweight show hunter, let alone breed one, as they are few and far between; this is most definitely reflected in the show ring, not only in the fact that it is usually the smallest class but also because many of the exhibits on show are often big common horses with unbalanced rounded action (and would be the first to tire out hunting). They hit the ground with their heels and cannot go fast enough at gallop even to catch a cold; they are very similar to the vanners of the cob world. However, the top-class heavyweight show horse is a rare treat to the eye. Although he may not be as agile a mover at trot nor as speedy at the gallop as the lightweight or middleweight, he is the flagship of the fleet.

Fig 30 Sporting Print, Small Hunter of the Year 1973 by Little Cloud and owned by the Countess of Inchcape, who gave the horse to Vin Toulson who in turn gave him to his head girl Jean Andrews (seen here) for whom he won the title again in 1975.

The small hunter class became popular after the war when the smaller, more active type of horse was in demand. Although there is a mixture of types in this class, the ideal is a miniature middleweight: small, compact and up to weight without being cobby and able to operate like his bigger brothers. This type of horse is easier to feed and produce and is ideal for the young or smaller rider who does not want to compete in hacks or could not possibly cope with a heavy-/middleweight horse.

At one time the class had an age limit for riders, and exhibits also had to jump, which does not happen today. It is a real pity that only a few shows allow the small hunter into the Championship, as in some years the small hunter winner is outstanding and would be worthy of the Champion Ridden Hunter title, as was the case when Small Print won it at City of Leicester in 1989 and Statesman was Champion at the RIHS in 1985.

The horse that does not necessarily fit into a specific weight category, can compete very successfully in novice, four-year-old, ladies', and working hunter

*Fig 31   Goodwill, Working Hunter of the Year 1969, by
Evening Trial. HRH The Princess Royal rode him in the 1976
Olympic Three-Day Event.*

classes. In the novice class, and particularly in the four-year-old class, the judge will allow for a certain amount of greenness (as some horses do take longer to mature in their ride and performance than others), providing they are going pleasantly and are not too ill-mannered. The wise owner will not overshow his young ridden animal but use these classes as an occasional 'school'. The ladies' hunter (which is more often than not ridden side-saddle) can be a lighter, smaller type of hunter, but must have impeccable manners with smooth, comfortable, well balanced paces.

The working hunter class is very popular with the one-horse owner who prefers to ride in many disciplines and wishes his horse to be judged on perfor-mance rather than just on personal opinion. He may have a horse that just misses being top class as a straightforward weight horse, possibly due to showing a blemish or a little wear on the joints (but if a good weight horse jumps and performs as well, the judge will obviously prefer this). Some horses are produced solely for this class, others use this class as a stepping stone with other equestrian spheres in mind. Eventers such as Castlewellan (Working Hunter of the Year 1979), Andeguy (Working Hunter of the Year 1981), Persian Holiday and Goodwill, (Working Hunter of the Year 1969), all competed successfully in Working Hunter Classes, as did Upton (Working Hunter of the Year 1970), who as Sanyo Video won the King

George V Gold Cup with Robert Smith. Roy Trigg's Morning Glory who was Working Hunter of the Year in 1976, jumped successfully to Grade A status with Derek Ricketts; and David Broome's Sportsman also competed in working hunter classes early in his career. In one week, Mary Gordon Watson's eventer Cornishman won a novice event at Sherbourne, the working hunter class at Royal Windsor and his first three-day event at Tidworth.

Similarly, some producers also use the show classes to train horses for other disciplines: Roy Trigg who started showing when he was nine years old and is an outstanding top showman, for many years also broke racehorses for many top trainers including Guy Harwood, John Dunlop and Captain Ryan Price, who had him show some horses prior to racing them, which Roy believed contributed greatly to their education before chasing.

Devon Pilgrim, who won a lot of three-mile chases, won the middleweight class at Richmond Royal under the name of Aintree; and Lord Belper's Alcore, who won several good chases, won the four-year-old class at the Royal. Roy also showed several of H.M. The Queen Mother's horses including Brig-o-Dee who became a police horse after racing. Some show horses even become television stars: Swanbourne who was an outstanding winner of both lightweight and middleweight show hunter classes, regularly appears in Yorkshire Television's 'Emmerdale Farm' series!

Hunter of the Year at The Horse of the Year Show from 1949			
1949	Mighty Fine	1970	Top Notch
1950	Mighty Atom	1971	Admiral
1951	Mighty Atom	1972	Admiral
1952	Rajah III	1973	Princes Street
1953	Penny Royal	1974	Aristocrat
1954	Cufflink	1975	Langton Orchid
1955	Mighty Grand	1976	Bally Manor
1956	Mighty Grand	1977	Bunowen
1957	Gowran Boy	1978	Bunowen
1958	Silverin	1979	Flashman
1959	Toby	1980	Brigadier
1960	Gold Dust	1981	Bayleaf III
1961	Swagger	1982	Assurance
1962	Viking	1983	Elite
1963	Romeo VI	1984	Seabrook
1964	Romeo VI	1985	Standing Ovation
1965	Spey Cast	1986	Seabrook
1966	Monbra	1987	Seabrook
1967	Tudor Line	1988	Classic Tales
1968	State Visit	1989	Mr. Meade
1969	Top Notch		

N.B. Hunters had lightweight and heavyweight classes from 1955 to 1959; from then on they were judged in three weight categories.

Riding Horses

Despite much opposition, riding horse classes were first staged at Harringay in 1955. They proved to be very popular, although the problem was that they took too long to judge as the accent was definitely on action and competitors were expected to perform all sorts of tests, even to open gates. Unfortunately, these were abandoned and did not return to the Horse of the Year arena until 1986 as the popularity of the classes demanded a representation at this level. The success of these classes and the impact that the riding horse – no longer considered to be bridesmaid to the hack – has had on the showing scene is surely reflected in the fact that four years later, Fair Breeze, a riding horse which I produced, took the Champion of Champions award beating the established models such as the hunter, hack, cob, pony, small hunter and working hunter at the 1989 Horse of the Year Show.

Nowadays, the classes are judged as normal showing classes (although at some unaffiliated shows, the entries may still be asked to jump a small fence) and divided into two sections: the small class,

Fig 32   Fair Breeze, Riding Horse of the Year 1989 and winner of the Champion of Champions award. Produced by the author and ridden by Nigel Hollings.

Fig 33   Burroprince, Riding Horse of the Year 1987 and 1988, shown by Alister Hood who said, 'He was magic to ride when right, but would often be electric'.

up to 15.2hh, which suits most riders; and the large class, over 15.2hh, which at present does not have an upper height limit and gives the horse that may have been too light for the hunter class, a show class to compete in. The possible need to enforce a height limit has been discussed at committee level for a couple of years now because, while the small class has quickly established a true type, the large one still has a vast range of mixtures. In conclusion, it was felt that for a while anyway, it should be left for the judges to decide which type they preferred; often, the judge's preference is not governed by height anyway since some of the best models can be 16.2hh plus and the more hunter types considerably smaller.

The true riding horse has been described in many different ways: the type of horse that would be up to the weight of the average person and that you would enjoy riding all the time, a hack of hunter type, and a covert hack. The society recommends, however, that judges should choose a horse that is between a hack and a hunter; one that does not require the elegance of the former nor the substance of the latter.

In a hack class, the individual show is of

Fig 34 Layton Ambassador, produced by the author to win the
large riding horse class at the RIHS in 1989, on his way to
winning a one-day event at Belton.

extreme importance; not so in the riding horse class under some judges. In fact, if pushed for time, you may not be asked to do one, simply because the ride is the most important aspect of the class and most judges will attempt to ride all the exhibits instead.

The riding horse will be expected to be as well schooled as a hack, although not as light and extravagant in way of going, but with a bolder attitude and able to gallop without becoming uncontrollable. Too many riders gallop too fast, which is unsightly. To be correct, the pace should be a hand gallop, something between a canter and a gallop; galloping was not allowed in the park in the old days and the hand gallop was the fastest permitted pace.

Riding Horse of the Year at The Horse of the Year Show

1955	Burrough Hills	1988	Burroprince
1986	Meridian	1989	Fair Breeze
1987	Burroprince		

Show Ponies

Unique is a word that springs to mind when describing our lovely show ponies, whose production and presentation far exceeds any other show animal. Although some awful sights can be viewed (often when a young jockey is completely over-horsed because mother and father have purchased the wrong pony), the general standard is so high that very few stars emerge from the classes because the top six in most classes can be differently placed from show to show depending on how they perform on the day and on the merest whim or fancy of the judge in the middle of the ring; in the past, quite often, only the first two were of quality and then the class tailed off.

The demand for a quality pony is not just a modern-day reality. Many of the exhibits in the early days of Olympia were by Thoroughbreds, often small polo pony sires. Mrs K. V. Coate's Kavora Kismet, which was winning such a lot in 1938 and 1939, was a typical example, being by a Thoroughbred teaser owned by Lord Rank, Mrs Coates' brother.

After the war it was the grey stallion Naseel by Raftan, ex Naxeena, bred by the late Gladys Yule who made a great impact on the ridden pony world. This was largely because ponies bred by Mrs Nicholson at Kells in Co. Meath, particularly Pretty Polly, My Pretty Maid and Eureka, all by Naseel, ex Gypsy Gold (who was by the Thoroughbred Good Luck, ex a Welsh mare Tiger Lily), won at all the major shows in the early fifties. Nowadays, hardly any of our top show ponies originate from Ireland; instead many from England make the journey across there, often bought very cheaply.

Fig 35   Runnings Park Hill Star, Pony of the Year 1982, produced and co-owned by the author. Seen here ridden by Emma Hilton collecting the Rawnsley Cup from Mrs Edna Hunnable, after winning the Championship at the RIHS.

When holding a seminar there, on noticing the overwhelming enthusiasm for the sport, I asked why no one bothered to buy the best English animals to improve the standard. I was told that there would be no point because as soon as, say, a £4000 pony arrived in Ireland it would be devalued by 50 per cent automatically.

The legendary Pretty Polly made her debut as a ridden pony at Dublin in 1949, ridden by Barbara Falloon. The judge who made her Champion, the late Horace Smith, thought then that 'she was an outstanding pony although shown by too large a jockey who covered her up'. His only doubts were that she may have been too small to win in England as she

Fig 36   Enoch Arden by Ardencaple, Show Pony of the Year 1958.

was only 13.3hh and that she did need to make up quite a bit – not unlike any other four-year-old.

The following May she was Champion at the Royal Ulster Show and, later on, was purchased by the late Albert Deptford to be shown in England and to be produced by the Lee-Smith family. The rest is history. She swept all before her and was to win the Pony of the Year title at Harringay for the next two seasons. The following year, 1951, Mr Deptford bought her four-year-old sister, the 13.2hh My Pretty Maid who had won at the Dublin Spring Show. She finished Reserve Champion to Polly at the RIHS White City that year; she was also accompanied in the winners' enclosure by her elder full brother Eureka

Fig 37   Second Thoughts, Show Pony of the Year 1961. The first ever 12.2 hh pony to win this award.

Fig 38   Royal Show, Pony of the Year 1952 and 1956, ridden by Jennie Bullen, now Loriston-Clarke. The only pony to beat Pretty Polly (at Aldershot and RIHS).

ding in 1953 or 1954), twice Champion at Royal Windsor, three times Champion at Richmond Royal, Peterborough, NPS and White City. She remained unbeaten until the RIHS in 1953 when, under Major Faudel-Phillips, she was vanquished both in her class and the Championship by the six-year-old gelding, Royal Show, ridden by the young Jennie Loriston-Clarke (née Bullen). The more robust Royal Show (who was Pony of the Year in 1952 and 1956 and Champion at the RIHS again in 1955) was bred in Lincolnshire by the late William Benson, and was by the polo pony sire Grey Metal, ex Flash III.

In 1954, Polly's final year, she was produced by the Harries family and

who, ridden by Janet Richardson, finished second Reserve, having been runner-up to Polly in the 14.2hh class. Similarly, in the Championship at the Horse of the Year Show later in the season, this group were to the fore again. Polly was naturally Champion, with Eureka Reserve and Maid second Reserve this time.

It must have been a gratifying moment for Mrs Nicholson who came over from Ireland to witness a brother and two sisters, bred by her, completely dominate the Championship at the two most prestigious shows. It was a remarkable achievement even by present-day standards and one which must be every breeder's dream.

Polly, in her career, was twice Champion at Harringay (not being allowed to compete in 1952 owing to a rule barring the previous year's winner and not atten-

Fig 39   Holly of Spring, Pony of the Year 1975, 1976, 1977 and 1978, with Camilla Hall in the saddle, who showed her after Brigit Ensten and before Cathryn Cooper. The author's brother was in fact the first person to sit on her at Davina Whiteman's yard.

*Fig 40   Creden Lucky Charm, Pony of the Year 1964,
ridden by Judy Bradwell, in the collecting ring at the Great
Yorkshire show after winning the Championship there.*

ridden by Christine Harries who had ridden My Pretty Maid the previous year when Mr Deptford sold her to Mrs Coates of 'Kavora' fame. Lightly shown, Polly won the Championship at the Royal held in Windsor Great Park and the RIHS, where she avenged Royal Show who beat her again at Aldershot that year.

As a brood-mare she has repaid the Deptford family many times over. Her progeny have included My Pretty Lady, Cusop Policy, Jenny Wren, Polly Flinders, Polly Perkins, Polyanthus, Polly's Aster and Polly's Gem who went straight to stud and produced Gem's Signet, Pony of the Year in 1971 and Reserve in 1973, and sire of Holly of Spring, four

times Pony of the Year. Perhaps the most famous of her offspring was Pollyanna who was sold to America for £8,000 (a record sum), by Mr Deptford, after a much garlanded career which included Reserve Pony of the Year in 1962 and the Championship in 1963.

With Polly retired, My Pretty Maid continued to uphold the family honour: she was Pony of the Year in 1955 (a repeat of 1953), often beating Royal Show, her sister's only vanquisher. In the three seasons Mrs Coates owned her, she was only beaten once in her class with two Windsor and two Richmond titles under her belt.

The small Thoroughbred Ardencaple was the next influential stallion and pro-

Fig 41   Treharne Veronica, Pony of the Year 1970, ridden by Susan Anne Rose and produced by Colin Rose, who said 'she was my biggest winner'.

duced, amongst many others, Ponies of the Year Enoch Arden and Arden Tittle Tattle. The next stallion to make his mark was the legendary Bwlch Valentino who sired Pollyanna, Creden Lucky Charm, Treharne Veronica, Snailwell Charles, Cusop Quickstep and Cusop Pirouette, and who stood at the famous Cusop Stud belonging to the Eckley family. Born in 1950 and bred by the late Nell Pennell, Bwlch Valentino was by Valentine (who was by the American champion polo pony sire Malice) ex Bwlch Goldflake whose sire was a Thoroughbred called Meteoric (a son of Derby winner Sun Star). Goldflake's dam was Cigarette, reputed to be the fastest 13hh pony of her day as she won most of her Galloway races of 1½ miles for 13hh ponies in South Wales and

border meetings. A bronze model of 'Val' is presented as a trophy to the breeder of the Pony of the Year at Wembley. Then followed his son Bwlch Zephyr (a grandson of Kavora Kismet and the sire of Favourita) and, in turn, his son Bwlch Hill Wind, who has sired such ponies as Rosevean Eagles Hill, Gem's Signet, Trellech Giselle and Runnings Park Hill Star. The progeny of these three stallions dominated the pony scene for over twenty years and many of the Champions of today have Valentino in their pedigree.

Before the 1930s, the height divisions for the show ponies were 12hh, 13hh and 14hh, after which there were no set classes as such since most shows varied although the most popular classes were up to 13hh and 13hh to 14.2hh. When the

BSPS was founded in 1949, with the help of such people as John Tilling and Brigadier Allen, the height divisions were rigidly enforced as they are today 12.2hh, 13.2hh and 14.2hh.

The 12.2hh class is the smallest of the three open classes, and is for riders up to twelve years of age. Although this type of pony shows more native blood than his larger colleagues, he should be more quality than the first ridden type and be bolder and more elegant in his way of going; he will also be expected to push

on in canter, if not to gallop for a few strides.

The 13.2hh class, like the middle-weight hunter, should be the model type: neither native like the 12.2hh nor horsey as can sometimes be seen in the 14.2hh class. The age limit is up to and including fourteen years of age and so the judge expects a polished display with a pony being shown well in all of the paces. The 14.2hh class is interesting to watch as there can be two types on show: a stronger made, up to height one, possibly

Fig 42   Cusop Pirouette, Pony of the Year 1966. This 12.2hh mare by Bwlch Valentino stood above 13.2hh stable companion Whalton Caprice in the Championship judged by Cynthia Haydon and H. Llewelyn Richards, a notable double for the Gilbert Scott family.

Fig 43   Ocean So Fair, Pony of the Year 1979 and winner of the 12.2hh class at Wembley five times in all – surely a record!

of horsey type; and a smaller, very pony type, just over 14hh, who may not cover the ground as well – consequently, one can more often detect a judge's preference for type in this class than in another. Even though many children seem to be bigger these days and the demand for the larger pony is far greater than supply, the schedule also includes the lighter-framed, smaller pony who should not be ignored when judging, even if he is not your favourite type.

Although the wording of the schedule no longer includes the guideline 'suitable to be ridden by', some judges will still accept slight exuberance in this class for jockeys up to sixteen years of age, where-

as in the smaller height classes, ponies have to be absolutely bombproof. One reason this class is one of my favourites, having produced such winners as Runnings Park Hill Star, Gay Sovereign, Rumour, Towy Valley Chiff Chaff and Tomatin Forest Wind to name but a few, is that the jockeys ride very well, like young adults, with elegance, style and authority.

When judging novice classes, nothing pleases me more than seeing a young pony who has the makings of an open Champion. Unfortunately, too many will never improve beyond the novice stage, and are usually a product of the overspill of indiscriminate breeding poli-

*Fig 44   Arden Vol au Vent of Creden, a big winner of 12.2 hh
show pony classes, including four times at the RIHS, pictured
here with Mandy Forster in the Championship. Behind are
14.2 hh winner Gems Signer (far right) and Snailwell Charles
(middle), the 13.2 hh winner at the BSPS Championship Show
1974.*

cies. I do not like to see three-year-old ponies being shown in these classes, which is allowed after July 1st, just as I feel sad when a good young pony is over-shown, winning novice classes every weekend throughout the season. The purpose of novice classes is to give an owner an opportunity to educate more slowly a young pony who may still be too green to compete successfully in the more demanding open classes. Having said that, some experts believe that a pony should stop at home until he is

ready to compete in open classes, believing that he is either ready for the ring or not. As a judge, if ever I am confronted with a situation where a pony with bags of potential, who has not gone well, is tying for first place with a pony who has gone only slightly better on the day but whose future I feel will be shortlived, I will go for the former, hoping that he will reach dizzy heights and I can proudly say that I was the first to judge the pony and reward his potential.

The restricted open classes (for ponies

Fig 45   Christmas Carol of Bennochy,
Pony of the Year 1974, pictured after
winning the Championship at Devon
County with Ruth Illsley on board. He
qualified for the Fredericks as a yearling
at the Royal Highland Show.

all starting the juvenile riders class (animals up to 15hh and riders up to eighteen years of age) in which I prefer the pony bred small hack type (the show hunter type and heavier made pony already being catered for in other classes). The BSPS also introduced experimental intermediate classes for horses up to 15.2hh and riders from eighteen up to twenty-five. Even though these classes have received much criticism from the pony-breeding intelligentsia, they have proved their worth and will help the young adult rider to adjust to larger animals in a more welcome environment (providing the judges ask more from them by expecting a higher standard of training and riding) before venturing into the big wide world where, in many cases, they will have to compete against the professionals who train them. However, not every young

that have not recently qualified for the RIHS or HOYS) which are so popular at the BSPS Championship Show, give the open pony who may not have Wembley potential a chance to compete successfully at his own level. As well as providing a suitable stepping stone for the novice pony who is ready to take to a double bridle later in the season, it gives owners a chance to test the water and see if they have an open pony in the making for the following year.

Whereas the horse showing societies have done very little to encourage the teenage rider (although at the time of writing, the BSHC&RHA is planning to hold suitable classes at its National Championships Show), the BSPS have made great strides in this area by first of

Fig 46   Lennel Aurora, Pony of the
Year 1973, exhibited by the Gilbert
Scotts who, in the opinion of the author,
are the best producers of ridden ponies
in the business.

57

*Fig 47   Gunnerby Aalborg Elegant, Pony of the Year 1981
(seen here as a brood-mare). Being pink roan she proved that
any colour can win if the pony is good enough.*

rider may wish to use this stepping stone section, especially if he believes that the only way to learn is to go in at the deep end.

At the other end of the age range, there are the lead rein classes, which, at some shows, are divided into two sections: up to 11.2hh; and 11.2hh to 12hh. These classes are for riders up to and including seven years of age and so cater for the various sizes of small children. There is a great art in presenting the lead-rein pony (although at times it looks as though the mother has spent more time and trouble on her own outfit at the expense of the pony's looks), and matching the size of the jockey to the pony so that there is no imbalance is a major consideration.

As the standard of production reaches an all-time high, more judges are stripping these ponies in order to separate the exhibits. However, even though stripping gives the team of handler, jockey and pony an additional test, this conformation phase is still not as important, in my opinion, as manners and way of going.

As the name of the class suggests, the lead rein (which should be attached to the noseband and not to the bit) acts as a safety cord and many judges, including me, prefer to see the handler doing very little. Of course, this must depend on the capability of the jockey but the handler should certainly not hold the pony back from flying off at trot or drag the pony out of line. Instead, the ideal picture is one

*Fig 48   Weston Velvet, owned by Mrs
E. Wiggins and ridden by Ami
Wiggins at the BSPS International Pony
Championships in 1987. A delightful
picture of a winning lead-rein combination.*

of the jockey being safely accommodated
by the pony who has a good front and is
not too wide, is extremely well mannered
and whose paces are smooth – the stride
being neither too choppy nor too long.
The lead rein class is a delightful class to
watch and should be an enjoyable way of
introducing a child to showing as well as
giving him confidence in the ring.

It is very important that the right pony
is found for the jockey, which applies
even more so in the first ridden class
when the jockey is expected to be more
advanced than a mere passenger. For
ponies up to 12hh (and riders who must
not have reached their ninth birthday
before 1st January of the current year)
the ideal is one who goes freely forward

*Fig 49   Chancley Tinkerbell, a good type of first ridden
pony, pictured winning at Newark & Notts in the capable
hands of eight-year-old Louisa Clarke.*

and is scopier in all ways than the lead-rein pony, capable of smooth transitions (cantering is expected in the individual show) and with good steering. As this is the first time a jockey is riding independently (although members of the family are usually dotted at regular intervals outside the ringside to offer assistance), manners are extremely important; however this does not mean the judges like to see children constantly flapping their legs at their ponies to make them go faster than a boring plod around the ring.

Of all the ridden pony classes, perhaps the most enjoyable to compete in are the pairs classes and great fun can be derived from matching everything down to the last detail. To begin with, make sure the basic picture of pony and jockey is harmonious and that the ponies' length of stride is similar. Two more important points to remember are that one of the jockeys must be in charge and decide when to canter, when to rise to the trot and so on; and if one pony has a slightly longer stride, which can sometimes be more noticeable at canter, place him on the outside for most of the time, i.e. on the right rein.

I have produced two successful pairs in recent years: a pair of dun ponies, Downland Smuggler and Sinbad of Pendle, who won at Royal Windsor and the BSPS Championships; and another pair, which many people said were the best pair they have ever seen, Gay Sovereign and Perryditch March Winds who won at the RIHS in 1980.

Pony of the Year at The Horse of the Year Show from 1949

1949	Legend	1970	Treharne Veronica
1950	Pretty Polly	1971	Gems Signet
1951	Pretty Polly	1972	Snailwell Charles
1952	Royal Show	1973	Lennel Aurora
1953	Kavora My Pretty Maid	1974	Christmas Carol of Bennochy
1954	Hassan	1975	Holly of Spring
1955	Kavora My Pretty Maid	1976	Holly of Spring
1956	Royal Show	1977	Holly of Spring
1957	Kavora Mr. Crisp	1978	Holly of Spring
1958	Enoch Arden	1979	Ocean so Fair
1959	Arden Tittle Tattle	1980	Kateslea Zindle
1960	Arden Tittle Tattle	1981	Gunnerby Aalborg Elegant
1961	Second Thoughts	1982	Runnings Park Hill Star
1962	Cusop Quick Step	1983	Harmony Bubbling Champagne
1963	Pollyanna	1984	Coveham Fascination
1964	Creden Lucky Charm	1985	Twylands Carillon
1965	Shandon	1986	Gaylord of Keston
1966	Cusop Pirouette	1987	Groundhills Amazing Grace
1967	Favourita	1988	Creden Keepsake
1968	Greenacres Twilight	1989	Jackets Maysong
1969	Shandon		

N.B. In 1955, there were two classes: up to 13.2hh and 13.2hh to 14.2hh. In 1957, three height classes were introduced.

Working and Show Hunter Ponies

Whereas the show pony could be considered by some to be impractical, the working hunter/show hunter pony is far from it and can compete in many other competitions with equal success. Having said that, we used to hunt our show ponies during the winter months and all the HOYS qualified ponies experienced cub hunting the week before Wembley.

The ideal is a miniature of our show hunter, preferably middleweight or heavyweight with good conformation, limbs with good flat bone and showing an ability to gallop really well. The description of hunters on pages 38–40 is also applicable in this case although one still wishes to see some pony characteristics, which are missing at times in the 15hh section. There are three height sections: 13hh, 14hh and 15hh, for riders up to fourteen, sixteen and eighteen respectively; there is also a class for 12hh ponies, for riders up to eleven years of

Fig 50 Whittaker's Lord, Show Hunter Pony of the Year in 1985, ridden by Lorraine Tatlow. This versatile 15hh animal had previously been shown with success as a small hunter and cob.

Fig 52   Downland Smuggler (14hh), a prolific winner of WHP Championships, produced by the author. 'He gave you 100 per cent at every show'. Together with Sinbad of Pendle, he also won the pairs class at the Royal Windsor, BSPS Wales and BSPS Championship Shows.

Fig 51   Towy Valley Moussec, a good stamp of a 13hh show hunter pony. Produced by the author to win many Championships, seen here after winning the Ponies UK Hunter Pony of the Year title.

age, and it is this last class which is one of the most difficult to judge since there is such a mixture of shapes and sizes.

In an ideal world, there should not be alarming differences in type between the working hunter pony and the show hunter pony, although a little wear and tear may be acceptable in the former classes. The best and easiest way to assess these ponies is to imagine what the animal would look like blown up into a horse and whether it would then meet the basic requirements.

I have enjoyed producing these ponies as they have fitted in well alongside our show horses and I feel that a healthier respect for sound conformation and feet is more in evidence in these classes than in the show ponies, possibly because many of the judges come from hunting, racing

and eventing backgrounds. It is true to say that horsemen rather than pony exhibitors are far more aware of the advantages of good conformation and of how faults can lead to unsoundness.

Some pony judges are not riding people and are only aware of weaknesses from reading books, which allows only a limited knowledge. The danger is that a judge whose knowledge is mainly theoretical may not be able to assess the gravity of a fault, depending on its location and size. For instance, a splint can at times be overlooked if it is not too pronounced and does not impose on the tendon. Similarly an unknowledgeable judge will not be able to differentiate between a horse that is a high blower and a horse that makes a noise. Experience, it is said, will make fools wise.

Fig 53   Runnings Park Brut (14hh), Show Hunter Pony Champion at RIHS 1987.

Show Hunter Pony of the Year at The BSPS Championship Show			
1983	Seaway Panther	1987	Upton Raparee
1984	News Extra	1988	Chirk Clwyds Lad
1985	Whittaker's Lord	1989	Kinlochmoidart
1986	Little Diamond		

3 Conformation

Once, when assessing entrants in a young judges competition, one of my questions was 'What is the object of breeding, finding or riding a horse or pony with good conformation?' Many said that an animal that is well made and has good basic framework will be pleasant to look at compared to an ugly-looking horse. Very few went a stage further by saying that there was a practical reason for this in that the horse or pony with good conformation will remain more sound and should be more comfortable to ride, whereas the one with alarming faults will be less efficient and put more strain on his structure.

The most perfect animal has not been found; he is a product of an owner's imagination. When judging, one can always find faults but the judge's ordeal is to weigh up the good and bad points and compare his assessment with each exhibit in the line.

It is important to remember that rules of conformation can vary depending on the type of horse. For instance, the conformation of the shire horse with his more upright shoulder suited to carrying a collar and designed for slower work, is markedly different to that of the average race horse whose build is designed more for speed and agility.

In theory, a horse that is beautifully proportioned with natural, balanced paces should be easier to produce for the ring, although there are some exceptions to this rule and one often sees a horse with conformation faults going like a Champion and winning prizes, for whatever reason. Perhaps it is because he may have an exceptionally good temperament, bags of quality and oozes presence – three ingredients which the Champion should have in abundance in addition to good conformation.

Quality is frequently referred to, but is difficult to define — the dictionary says that it is a degree of excellence. In horses, it means good as opposed to common breeding and is usually noticeable in the refinement of the head, coat and limbs. One of the best words which also sums up the meaning quite well is 'class'; just as a person with class is not necessarily good looking, so a person with perfect looks may lack that quality of class.

Coupled with this is the word presence: something which compels you to notice an animal straight away and not for the wrong reasons (flashiness or over-exuberance). In human terms, the best word to describe it is personality or individuality.

Temperament (which can be spoiled through bad management, either by mishandling or bad breeding), is also indirectly related to conformation in that it may be physically impossible for a horse to perform in the manner expected of him, which causes him to be irritable and resistant.

When assessing a horse's conformation, I stand back and look at the overall picture, which should be balanced with everything in proportion (*see* Fig 54). In this way, I can observe whether the

64

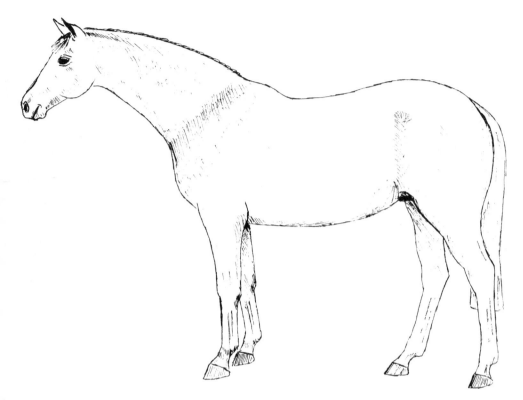

Fig 54 A picture of good, balanced conformation.

animal is long, herring-gutted, too big in the body for his limbs, short of croup or higher behind than in front, which gives a downhill ride (this is often seen in young-stock and improves with maturity). Similarly, a horse that is higher in front with the hind end dipping away will give an uphill ride, especially at trot.

As a strong believer in the saying, 'no foot, no horse', I will then look at the feet and, working upwards, examine the limbs, paying particular attention to the foreleg before starting on the head and working backwards. Before standing in front of and behind the horse, prior to asking the exhibitor to walk away from me in a straight line, I analyse the hind leg once more.

Just as a high-rise building needs a good foundation in order to remain standing, so a horse needs four good, strong and open feet to support his entire weight. What use is a good-looking horse if he is permanently unsound through bad, narrow and upright feet *(see* Fig 55)? In front and behind, feet should be a matching pair (although the hind feet are slightly smaller and more oval than the front ones). One of a pair should definitely not be smaller than the other, which is more commonly seen in front, and they must be of normal size, in proportion to the animal (small and boxy feet are bad, especially in deep going, and are often liable to develop navicular disease and sidebones; the animal with over large feet

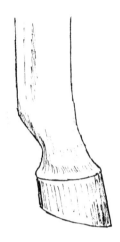

Fig 55   A narrow, upright foot.

1. Carbohydrate / protein overload which is the most common cause.
2. Toxaemia, e.g. colic.
3. Mechanical – poor foot dressing.
4. Trauma – exercise on hard ground.
5. Stress – e.g. travelling.
6. Iatrogenic – vet applied.

Pasterns should be neither too short and upright (*see* Fig 56a), nor too long and sloping (*see* Fig 56b). Short, upright pasterns cannot absorb concussion; this will have a tendency to stumble). Shallow flat feet make the animal tender over rough stoney ground, especially if shelly. The horn should be healthy and flint like, not brittle and breaking up at the edges or with cracks. The frog, which is the shock absorber in the foot, should be healthy and well developed, not shrivelled. Feet that have suffered from laminitis, a disease which most showing yards have experienced at one time or another, show signs of a dropped sole which often remains hypersensitive. The ridges produced on the hoof wall by laminitis are distinguishable from grass rings because they are more irregular and tend to merge towards the heel.

Laminitis   can affect all four feet and not just the front ones. I was always told that a horse with this condition should not be shod if the sole is concave, but if the sole is flat, it is best to shoe in order to give the frog some support. Some of the causes of laminitis are:

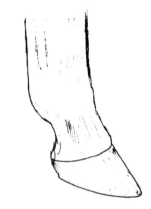

Fig 56(a)   A short, upright pastern.

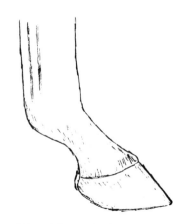

Fig 56(b)   A long, sloping pastern.

66

produces a jarring which results in an uncomfortable ride. Upright pasterns are often accompanied by upright shoulders. Long and sloping pasterns are usually accompanied by a straight hind leg and, as a result, are weak and place a great strain on the tendons. However, slightly long pasterns are said to give a more comfortable, springy ride. It is in this area that ring and side bones occur (low in the coronet region, high above the coronet). These are considered a fault.

The fetlock joint (the shock absorber) should be broad and give an impression of flatness rather than roundness. Puffiness in this region is a sign of strain and demonstrates that the animal is not up to much work, when he is said to be 'round of his joints'.

The cannon bone, which is equivalent to the human middle finger from the wrist to knuckle, should be short and strong, not long and narrow (denoting weakness). Nor should it become narrower just below the knee and hock when it is said to be 'tied in' when it is below the knee (see Fig 57a) and 'light of bone' when it is below the hock. This area between the fetlock and knee is of great importance. The circumference of bone determines the weight-carrying capacity of the horse and if the bone is flat and flint-like (showing no signs of roundedness or puffiness) and the tendons are clearly outlined, it can be described as quality limb. Thoroughbred quality bone has a greater strength and density than common bone, hence the old adage, 'An ounce of blood is worth an inch of bone'.

The knee should be large, flat and wide with a good surface area for muscles, ligaments and tendons. A well-developed trapezium bone at the back provides a good attachment area, but judges should be aware that this can sometimes make the bone below the knee look lighter than it really is.

The foreleg takes the strain of the horse's weight when he is active (particularly when jumping) and consequently, it is the most common site of lameness in the horse. It should be strong and well formed and straight from elbow to pastern. For a good length of stride, it is far better to have a long forearm and short cannon bone than the other way round.

If the leg bends slightly back from the knee (concave outline) this is called 'calf kneed' or 'back of the knee' (see Fig 57b). It is often seen in commoner breeds and is definitely considered a fault in the show ring. Legs of a concave shape are put at risk from strain. However a horse that is 'over at the knee' (see Fig 57c) (convex outline), rarely suffers from strained tendons. (In fact, many racing people prefer this formation to a normal foreleg) and providing it is not exaggerated and the animal does not look like a collapsible card table, it is not considered a fault in the show ring.

A free elbow is all-important and must not be set too close to the body, as this restricts the freedom of movement. A horse whose elbows are too close is said to be 'tied in at the elbow'.

The head, like the human face, can reveal the true character of the animal: too big a head looks common and unattractive; too small a one may indicate a mean nature, can make a horse look too ponyish and can cause teething and biting problems. Having said that, a good producer should be able to cover a bad head and a bad head is preferable to bad feet, limbs or hind legs, which are impossible to disguise and more troublesome. How-

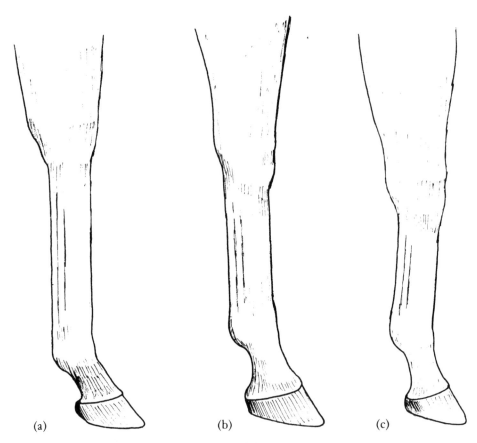

Fig 57(a)   *A long, weak cannon bone, 'tied in below the knee'.*
(b)   'Back of the knee'. (c) 'Over at the knee'.

ever, some people will not buy an animal unless it has a good head and they can look at it with appreciation. One lady once said that a horse her husband bought was so ugly that she had him moved to another stable so that she did not have to look at him from her kitchen window. More importantly, a big head which is out of proportion with the body will result in the horse being heavy in the hand and falling on his forehand; a rider has enough to do without carrying his horse's head as well.

Preferably, eyes should be large, bold and wide apart, placed to the front as much as possible with a kindly and intelligent expression, which is a good indication of his temperament (beware of the small piggy eye which looks back at you nervously). Ears can be just as informative about the character of the horse. They should be of average size, not turning inwards (because this may denote craftiness) and they should move as though having a conversation with you, not necessarily pointing permanently forward as if stitched and certainly not flat back. Judges should be aware of parrot mouths which are considered a fault due to biting and grazing problems in extreme cases. One leading judge once put a big winner down from the top spot at a show for this reason, after others had missed it! Judges that fiddle about in ponies' mouths to determine their age, because they do not believe the jockeys, can be a nuisance – particularly those who do not know what they are looking for in the first place, often frightening the ponies.

The neck should be set on well at both ends, running into a good sloping shoulder and well-defined wither. There should be a nicely curved, clean-cut junction between the head and the neck, otherwise there will be difficulty in asking the horse to flex (*see* Fig 58a) which could also lead to respiratory problems. The neck should be longer on the top side than underneath, forming a well-defined convex top line from poll to withers, so that the horse flexes at the poll and not lower down the neck. A horse that is ewe necked (upside-down necked) will give a strong and unbalanced ride (*see* Fig 58b). The neck should also be in proportion, giving a picture of balance with the rest of the horse: not too short, which gives the rider an awful feeling of insecurity and tends to make the horse carry his head high, often pulling the rider; nor too long which can affect the balance as the horse will have difficulty in carrying himself and the head.

Many people mistakenly believe that a good front is one that has a long neck or good length of rein. However, unless it is accompanied by a good shoulder, this is incorrect. Withers should be well formed and should neither be too high, which produces a high knee action, nor too low or flat (often accompanied by straight, upright shoulders), which tend to give a downhill ride and allow saddles to move forward. Withers should not be confused with shoulders as it is quite possible for a

Fig 58(a)   A short, stuffy neck.

(b)   'Ewe-necked'.

69

good wither to be accompanied by a straight shoulder.

A long sloping shoulder (approximately 55 degrees) will not only give an extended action, but also a facility for greater, freer action and therefore a better ride. The straight shoulder with its stilted action will produce the opposite. Lumpy-looking shoulders known as loaded shoulders often provide very jarring rides.

The riding animal should have a deep chest and a good girth line. If he lacks depth, he will be said to 'show a lot of daylight' and this denotes insufficient room for the heart and lungs to develop to their full capacity, although many youngsters that are leggy do deepen to some extent with maturity. The common thumb rule is that the lowest point of girth should be almost half-way between the top of the withers and the ground line. The girth line should always be deeper in front than behind if the saddle is to remain in the correct place. Likewise, if the animal tends to run up light beyond the saddle, it will be difficult to prevent the saddle from slipping back, apart from the fact that it will always look short of condition; this is called being 'herring-gutted' (see Fig 59a).

The back should be strong as this is the weight-bearing area of the horse. It should be slightly concave to afford a comfortable ride and run down from the wither over a well-muscled loin area to the croup, showing no signs of weakness. A hollow or dipped back (see Fig 59b), sometimes a sign of old age, is a weakness although it can still give a comfortable, 'slotted in' ride. The opposite condition, known as a hog or roach back (see Fig 59c), usually gives a bumpy ride. From a showing point of view, the horse with a

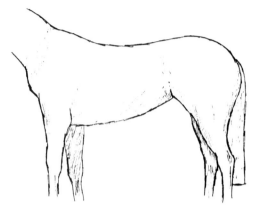

Fig 59(a)   'Herring-gutted'.

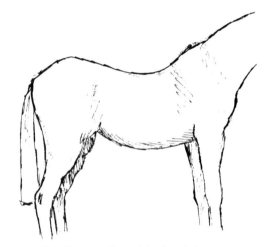

(b)   A hollow or dipped back, with sloping quarters and a low-set tail.

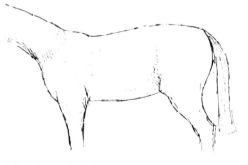

(c)   A roach back.

long back must be well muscled up to look less weak. A long back usually gives a good feel, because you are sitting in the middle of the horse, whereas the short backed horse, though stronger, can restrict the speed and action and is therefore less comfortable, giving the feeling that you are sitting on top of the engine.

The hindquarters are the engine room and the hind leg, the engine. I particularly like to see a good length of croup with a well set-on tail and definitely not quarters that are very flat or that slip away to a low-set tail (*see* Fig 59b), on which you can imagine there to be a sign saying 'Test your brakes'. A horse that carries his tail to one side or clamps it down, often has back trouble. The area should be well muscled and rounded with a strong, broad second thigh showing a good length from the hip bone to the point of hock, which indicates galloping ability.

Apart from the fact that all the power comes from the mechanics of the hind leg, another sound reason for having a strong hind leg is that it must be capable of bearing the full weight of the horse and rider over fences, just as the forearm takes the strain on landing. A correct hind leg incorporates a well-defined hock and illustrates the broom handle theory: when a horse is standing squarely, if a broom handle is held vertically from the point of buttocks, the point of the hock and back of the tendons to the ground should follow the same line.

Sickle hocks are considered a weakness (although some racehorse trainers believe that a horse will gallop well with sickle hocks, as they are naturally underneath the horse to begin with). The angle of the hocks is very acute and the hind legs are in the shape of a sickle (*see* Fig 60a). The more severe the angle the greater the

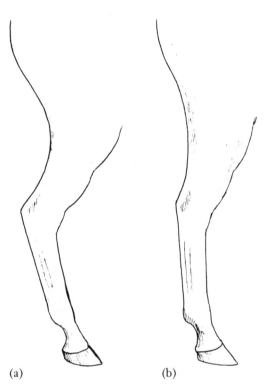

(a)   (b)

Fig 60   A sickle hock (a) and a straight hind leg (b).

weakness. Straight hocks are the opposite and result in a rather short stiff stride and a lack of flexion in the joint puts a strain on the hind legs. (*See* Fig 60b).

Weak or badly formed hocks are more susceptible to unsoundness caused by curbs; bog spavins (soft swellings on the front of the hock joint) and bone spavins found on the inside of the hock (*see* Fig 61). Thoroughpins, soft swellings found in the well of the hock, are also found in weak hock joints. If you come across any of these faults when judging, avoid touching them if possible, so that the rest of the ringside are not aware of what you have seen. If it is necessary to examine

71

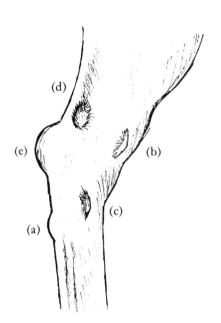

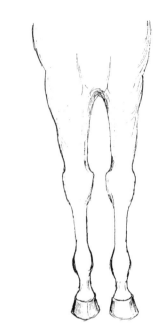

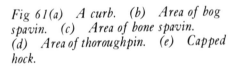

Fig 61(a)   A curb.   (b)   Area of bog spavin.   (c)   Area of bone spavin. (d)   Area of thoroughpin.   (e)   Capped hock.

Fig 62   A narrow chest.

further, do it to a few others to put the observers off the scent.

When looking at the horse from the front, the chest should not be too narrow, giving the impression that the forelegs emerge from the same hole (*see* Fig 62). A narrow horse will ride like a mountain peak, often moving close in front (usually plaiting) and will probably be a bad doer. A narrow chest is usually associated with a horse that is also lacking depth and is herring-gutted. Neither do you want to see a horse that is too broad in the chest (*see* Fig 63). This is often associated with the sprung-ribbed horse with loaded shoulders and gives a rolling feeling at canter and gallop, as it has a tendency to dish.

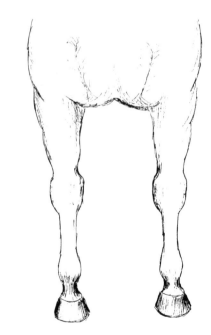

Fig 63   A bosomy chest.

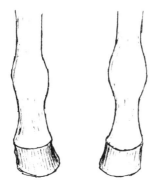

Fig 64(a)   'Pigeon-toed'.

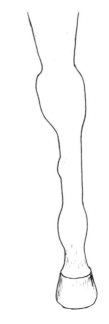

Fig 65   A splint on an off-set cannon bone.

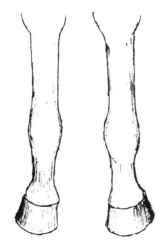

(b)   'Splay-footed'.

Feet should stand square and face straight forwards; common faults are feet turning in (pigeon-toed), shown in Fig 64a, or turning out (splay-footed), shown in Fig 64b. A horse that has the latter fault should be avoided, as it puts a strain on the back of the tendons, as well as running the risk of the horse catching himself when moving. Other faults to look out for are odd knees, off-set cannon bones (*see* Fig 65), and twisted forelegs.

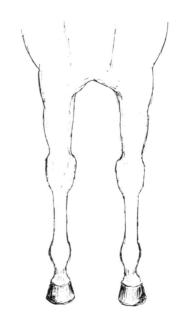

Fig 66   A front view of symmetry.

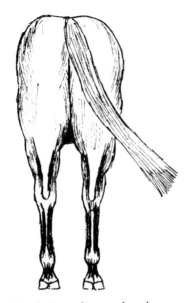

Fig 67   A back view of strength and squareness.

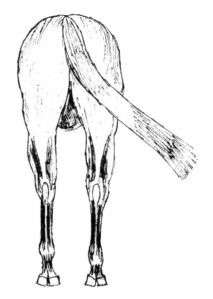

Fig 69   'Split up behind'.

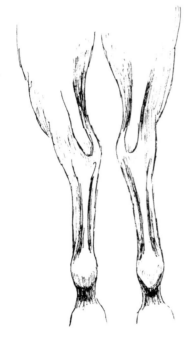

Fig 68   Cow hocks.

When looking from the front, a vertical line from the middle of the forearm should equally divide the foreleg. In theory, if an animal stands true, he should move straight; with a twisted foreleg, even if the horse does not throw it, there will be more strain on that joint. When standing behind the horse, one should usually see (as when looking from the front), a picture of strength, squareness and symmetry (*see* Figs 66 and 67).

Cow hocks are those that turn in, (*see* Fig 68), with the result that the horse often moves close behind. Barred hocks are the reverse: the hocks turn out and the toes turn in, causing the horse to go wide behind, which is unsightly. The expression 'being split up behind' describes poorly developed inside thigh muscles that leave space under the dock (*see* Fig 69). This is often accompanied by hocks in the air (as opposed to hocks that are well let down).

4   In Hand Showing

In hand showing is a very popular pastime and appeals to a wide range of people since it is within the capabilities of nearly everyone, whereas exhibitors with limited riding ability may only achieve limited success in the ridden show ring. Some much older exhibitors who used to take part in the ridden classes and hunt on a regular basis, possibly not being as active as they used to be and wishing to continue their interest, find much enjoyment in the more relaxed and less demanding confines of the in hand world. Others become involved quite unintentionally when it is decided to breed from a favourite mare which may have injured herself or has been outgrown by the children, (possibly past her best to move on to another home).

Even though the majority of people do not like to work with mares, it does at least give them another string to their bow and, in some cases, a mare can be more successful as a matron than a ridden exhibit. However, it must be said that there is a strong element of luck involved and it does not follow that the top-class mare will produce the best of foals. As the late Joe Massarella once said, 'You breed what God gives you, whereas you can buy what you want'. In some quarters, mares are considered to be more valuable, particularly if they have some very interesting bloodlines.

Unless geldings are retired at the top of their career, it is inevitable that they will gradually slip down the ladder and it is a particular pet hate of mine to see a former star propping up the line at a very mediocre show, looking like a shadow of his former self. Ideally, one would wish to find such a horse a good home as a companion to a youngster, but this is not an easy task.

When our pony Snailwell Charles had come to the end of his career, we bought him back and he spent the last years of his life turned away with Gem's Signet, at Mrs. Waddilove's home (Charlie's breeder). When they went to meet their maker, they were buried together, which was

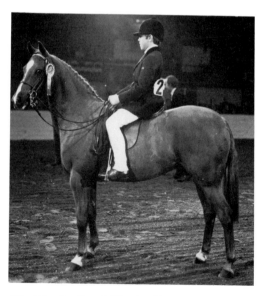

Fig 70   Snailwell Charles, Pony of the Year 1972 (and 13.2 hh Pony of the Year in 1973), ridden by the author's brother Nigel Hollings who, to date, is still the only boy to ride the Champion pony at the HOYS.

Fig 71   Gems Signet, Pony of the Year 1971 (and
Reserve 1973). The sire of Holly of Spring. Having
covered a few mares prior to being gelded, he was sold for
£8,000 to go under saddle. Pictured at Royal Windsor
Show (1971), his first major outing, where he was Champion
ridden by Sophie Waddilove.

very fitting as Gem was Pony of the
Year in 1971 and Charlie enjoyed similar
success the following year. In 1973 they
both fought for the Reserve Championship to Lennel Aurora, Gem getting the
verdict over Charlie who was second
Reserve.

One of my mares, Pendle Atalanta,
who bred Agar Heir Apparent (Hack of
the Year 1989) prematurely became a
'broody' following an accident in the
stable which left her with a damaged
hock. In fact, this did not affect her
success in the ring as a brood-mare.

Perhaps the most prominent group of

exhibitors in the in hand showing is the
commercial breeder, who views the show
ring as his shop window and a means of
promoting his stock and, in the majority
of cases, the resident stallion.

Over-Showing

The majority of in hand exhibitors love
to win rosettes and, because there are
more opportunities given to them these
days, they will think nothing of showing
youngsters and brood-mares and foals
two or three times a week during the peak

Fig 72   Pendle Atalanta, the author's small hunter mare ridden by Davina Whiteman, with whom the author trained for three years. The dam of 1989 Hack of the Year Agar Heir Apparent.

of the showing season, even in extreme weather conditions and, more foolishly, when brood-mares are on their three and six weeks, risking everything. In the past, the usual pattern was to show very little, but as a means of basic education: getting the horse accustomed to travelling in the horse-box, and becoming familiar with show ring conditions, as well as being trimmed and plaited up. This could entail showing once or twice as a foal, a few times as a yearling, nothing at two years of age and then just a few more outings as a three-year-old prior to breaking.

Although a list of in hand winnings will put value on the animal, (providing they are not all gained under the same judge) and read well in an advert in the

Fig 73   Agar Heir Apparent, Hack of the Year 1989. A very genuine horse, home-produced and ridden by owner David Cronk.

press and consequently impress some potential customers, the majority may be very wary, as it is generally thought that the answer to the question, 'Why is it that not many in hand animals make it under saddle?', is over-showing. In fact, many ridden purchasers prefer to buy an animal completely untouched.

Some youngsters in the in hand classes have seen more of our country than most human beings do by retirement age and this is not a good thing. Young developing limbs can be put under a lot of strain with excessive travelling (no matter how talented the horse-box driver), especially when adjusting their balance around corners and when stopping and starting, apart from the fact that loading and unloading on steep ramps also requires a great effort.

Gone are the days when youngsters could be shown at top-class level from the field, looking rangey and not in good coat. Many in hand animals are cooped up in an unnatural environment: rugged up all the time, sometimes under heat lamps and produced on corn feed, they are often too fat (covering up a multitude of sins although it can never convert a poor specimen into a good one), which is also bad for joints. Apart from the fact that their maturity is also being forced too quickly, leaving no room for further development in later years – only, possibly, upwards which results in the all too common sight of animals which are stuffy looking and lacking scope.

Over-showing can also lead to ring craftiness and nappiness which definitely puts a show animal at a disadvantage and, unless the producer for the next stage (under saddle) is very clever, that vital ingredient of a Champion, presence, will never be regained.

Many observers think that while the higher standard of production has greatly improved the ridden scene, it is having detrimental effects on the in hand world, simply because young animals are being over-produced. In a short space of time we have gone from seeing youngstock badly turned out and badly produced to seeing youngsters who look more mature than their years and going like saddle ponies to complement this — a case of production turning full circle.

How often do we see yearlings being worked on hard ground on show fields, trussed up like Christmas turkeys in tack with tight side reins, in an effort to give them this elevation of the ridden pony. What is actually happening is that these youngsters, apart from having their mouths ruined, are being forced into an unnatural shape, with a very swan-like front but a hollow back and, as a result, the natural balance is being altered. Even when an older animal is being ridden away, shortly after backing, the shape is lower and longer to begin with and it is not until the animal learns to work from behind and adapts more to the weight of the rider — a natural progression I might add – that we see the animal work in the correct, more elevated shape. People argue that Thoroughbreds are successfully raced at early ages, let alone schooled, but the facts are that they are usually fitter, having been hard fed from day one and are ridden in straight lines by lightweights, usually on turf.

If we overtravel, overfeed and overwork our youngsters, there will be nothing left for them to do; when the time comes for them to go under saddle, they will be empty shells. Surely the ultimate success of the breeder is to have bred an animal that has either become Pony of the

Year or won at Burghley, rather than just the best two-year-old at a major show.

Because the cost of breeding and caring for youngsters is increasing all the time and, economically, the breeding game is one big gamble, when a good pony is bred and a big cheque is offered, most breeders take the money. Although the short-term situation is very rewarding, such a pony who goes into the wrong home and does not fulfil expectations, could devalue the rest of your stock since he carries the same prefix. Although breeders, in my opinion, get very little recognition and not enough reward for all their hard work, I would ask them to consider taking less money at certain times, particularly if that youngster will have a better chance of succeeding, rather than just taking the biggest offer, which usually comes from a newcomer in the game. If the first youngster from a breeding line, bearing your prefix, reaches dizzy heights, there will be more chance of selling the rest of the stock, possibly for a lot more money. Although, having said that, brothers and sisters can be poles apart – another prime example of the inconsistency of the breeding game. However, the point I am trying to make is that this is yet another reason why some of our in hand prize winners do not make it under saddle: they sometimes go to the wrong type of home which cannot cope with highly strung, ringcrafty youngsters which can be likened to spoilt children.

Yet another reason is that to win in hand classes, some breeders are breeding the wrong type of animal – those that will not have the scope to perform under saddle, but do look pretty in the in hand classes. Ironically, these people are often the ones who find fault in other competitors' stock but are unable to see the folly of their own breeding policies. Time and time again we observe the fashionable yards producing stock full of quality but at the expense of substance and good limb. However, not all the blame should be laid at the feet of the breeder because if the judges did not favour these pretty but flimsy types, breeders would be forced to change their breeding programmes. After all, the judge's decision in the ring influences the development of type and breed.

Admittedly, it may be that the potential ridden types are not prominent in the youngstock classes for three reasons: the breeders are wise enough not to show them, looking to the future instead; they know that they will be unfashionable compared to the rest of the class and so it is not worth the effort to stand down the line (very rarely do we see judges put up only one of a type to win in a very large class); and also, some youngsters that will eventually be up to height ridden types are usually too big for the height requirements as laid down by the governing societies and therefore unable to be shown at the major shows, which is perhaps a blessing in disguise! Consequently, a judge can only place what is in front of him on the day and, again, if a well-presented animal deserves to beat a better ridden prospect which is not going or looking as well, then so be it. After all, showing is the name of the game and presentation should always be rewarded.

An expert once remarked that our English hunter judges seem to judge hunter breeding classes better when in Ireland. Could this be because the exhibits are not over produced and are therefore not tricking the judges in the same way, or because the animals on show are of a better stamp altogether?

In my opinion, it is ironic that the in hand and ridden worlds seem so far apart, as they should in theory complement each other. However, as one expert explained, this should not seem too ludicrous when we observe that the ridden animal is also judged on ride, performance and manners with conformation taking a varying percentage of the priorities depending on the judge. The in hand judge has to devote his energies totally to assessing correctness of conformation, particularly as it will be inevitable that some of these exhibits will be used for breeding either as colts or brood-mares and, anyway, he does not have the same facility to judge performance and movement as the ridden judge.

Ideally, the Champion should be correct in conformation but still show signs of having saddle potential. If they are light of bone and cannot stand up to work or do not have enough scope or length of stride to be comfortable to ride, they will simply be useless and unmarketable. Good limbs and feet, in my opnion, are far more important than pretty heads.

Breeding

In the horse world, a useful horse will always have a job of work, even if he does not match up to competition level. However, this is not the case in the pony world as many of them are too difficult to become an ordinary pony to an ordinary child and at the same time not good enough to win prizes at a reasonable level of competition. The proof of how the pony breeding situation has gone astray lies in the fact that, at the moment, we have a surplus of mediocre stock that no one wants at a time when the demand for the top-class ridden prospect has never been higher.

Breeders and breeding societies have the power in their hands to rectify this situation and reshape the showing scene. Breeders will need to adapt to meet the demand of the market in order to survive and societies could do no harm in inviting more performance people on to the panels and instructing judges to think more about the finished product.

Now that the NPS has formed an entirely separate hunter pony breeding judges panel, many exhibitors would like the riding pony breeding classification to be more specifically for show pony and show hunter pony breeding. Likewise, the hunter breeding exhibitors would like a separate range of classes introduced to cater for the young competition horse who often beats the true hunter type in the hunter breeding classes.

The in hand breeding scene has a major role to play in the showing world and an interesting situation has arisen involving the British Show Hack, Cob & Riding Horse Association which hopes that the new hack breeding classes will encourage exhibitors to breed the right type, which has gone missing from the ridden classes. Because the majority of its panel judges are ridden people, I believe there is every chance of this idea succeeding and less chance of what has happened in the pony and hunter world where, in each case, two different types of animal are being exhibited.

Brood-mares

The standard of brood-mares on show is excellent compared to the overall disap-

Fig 74 Kalya, a good stamp of hack brood-mare, owned by Mrs Noel de Quincey who is chairman of the British Show Hack, Cob and Riding Horse Association at the time of writing.

pointing display of youngstock, which could be the very reason the brood-mare often excels in a major Championship. The mare is the foundation of any breeding policy: 'like will produce like'. She has often proved herself under saddle before becoming a matron, which is more than can be said for many of the pony stallions. Joanna MacInnes has always placed much importance on the role of the dam, since a wise Thoroughbred breeder told her that the dam is responsible for 90 per cent of the influence and since the late Nell Pennell told her that she would never purchase a stallion until she had seen the mother. Some breeders, before using stallions, look back into the ances-

try, since what one expects to be a quality youngster can sometimes turn out to be a common brute if there is any common blood in the pedigree.

The ideal brood-mare is one whose basic conformation is good so that she does not pass on any obvious faults and unsoundness. She should stand over the ground on four good limbs and four good feet, be big and roomy, yet female with a kindly, generous outlook.

Stallions

When choosing a stallion, apart from looking at ways he will compensate for the mare's weaker areas, always look to

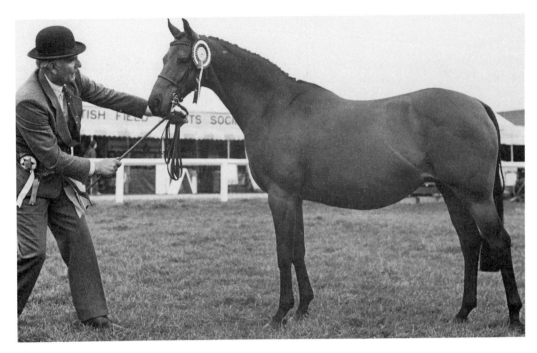

Fig 75   Trellech Giselle, many times Champion 13.2hh
brood-mare by Bwlch Hill Wind. In her showing career,
she qualified for the Lloyds five times, winning the pony section
in 1982 and 1987. Her daughter Rotherwood Rhapsody
qualified twice and won in 1985.

the future as well, i.e. look for ways of upgrading on the mare. Remember that standards are improving all the time; something which is winning under saddle in the early seventies may not even be looked at in the late eighties. It is common sense not to use a stallion with a weak hind leg if this is not your mare's strongest point or use a stallion that is light of limb and lacks scope and substance if the mare is of the same build. At times, mare owners feel obliged to use a friend's stallion, even though it may not be suitable, which is ridiculous as neither partner is doing the other a favour if the progeny is going to be a disaster. The unskilful or careless breeder will often so badly pair the animals that the good parts of each will be in manner lost, the defects of both will be increased and the produce will be far inferior to both sire and dam.

Whereas the hunter premium stallion and the Thoroughbred stallion have proved their worth in the performance field, many of the pony stallions have not and often their main attraction is the stock they produce. This leads to some pony stallions becoming fashionable, which is still not a good enough reason to use him on your mare if you know it will not work, although it is better ot use a stallion that is getting good stock rather than the opposite. It is possible that a good-looking stallion can produce mediocre stock while, sometimes, a moderate stallion can produce stock better than himself, yet another example of the gamble involved in breeding.

Another problem is that if you look at the bloodlines in the pony-breeding circle, there is a lot of line- and in-breeding, which can lead to bad temperaments. The traditionalists say that the temperament often comes through the sire. In explaining the difference between line-breeding and in-breeding, a top breeder once said jokingly, 'If the breeding policy works and the animal is good enough as regards temperament, conformation and so on, he is line-bred; but if it does not, he is in-bred.' In all fairness, it is wrong to put all the blame on the stallion as many of today's brood-mares are put in foal prematurely because their temperament is suspect in the ridden ring.

Joanna MacInnes who breeds the successful Whalton ponies looked at pony breeding lines a few years ago and, with advice from the late Glenda Spooner who owned Ardencaple, thought that the Thoroughbred outcross was worth trying. She added that if you believe in something, it is worth pursuing and as far as breeding is concerned, no matter which path you take and no matter how clever your educated guess, there is an element of chance involved. Another point to consider is that breeding should be looked upon as a long-term occupation: it may take two generations before you can hope to achieve your aim.

Interestingly enough, Elspeth Ferguson who has played a significant role in pony breeding circles, would look for a good small Thoroughbred stallion if she were to start all over again, especially to breed the bigger ponies to accommodate the bigger children. Thoroughbred pony stallions that were around in the early sixties included Golden Cross, Turtons Story, Grey Start, Chantain, Gay Presto and Ardencaple.

Some breeders believe that more pony character would be returned if a small Thoroughbred stallion was put to a pony mare rather than the other way round. Either way, using Thoroughbred blood is one way of achieving the right stamp with the good limb and quality which makes the Thoroughbred the envy of the world.

Production

Feeding and preparing mares for the show ring is a lot harder than people imagine because it is very rare that top-class shows can be won from the field. However, I do not think that mares should be kept in all the time with lots of rugs on; weather permitting, they should go out for between four and eight hours a day – after all, this is a natural activity. Small mares may need to have their grass restricted either by not going out for as long or by grazing on barer paddocks, in order to avoid weight problems or, possibly, laminitis.

Personally, I think that four to six shows a year is quite adequate for a brood-mare and foal if travelling long distances. Nowadays, with the standard of showing very high, mares must be hard fit which, without the help of ridden work, is difficult, but can be achieved successfully with good feeding and strapping.

Feeding is up to the individual but a guide to a good feeding system might include good quality hay, bran, sugar-beet, chaff and concentrates such as stud cubes and oats (depending on the mare), plus vitamins such as calcium, seaweed, multi-vit and linseed mashes three to four times a week (for the coat) together with a bran mash once a week.

For the first six to eight weeks, foals should be all right with mother's milk, and will probably be joining in with the mother in eating solids by then anyway. Be careful that the foal does not eat too well as this can lead to overheating, when foals are found to be rubbing their coats bald and sore. Sometimes, with first time and weaker foals, additional feeding may be necessary; though time consuming this will entail feeding the foal separately with the mare tied up. I have had great success with smaller feeds of foal creep nuts and bran, chaff and sugar beet.

Foals can be safely wormed at six weeks old and every six weeks after that. Many breeders worm the mares prior to foaling heat and then like to see the mares safely in foal before starting a serious worming programme.

It is generally understood that youngsters do most of their skeletal growing in the first twelve months; therefore, weaned foals are better kept up during their first winter having good quality nutritional food, paying particular attention to getting the calcium/phosphorous balance right. Bran is high in phosphorous but low in calcium and beet pulp is the reverse. Abnormal bone formation can be caused by a calcium/phosphorous imbalance and similar problems arise when bone formation is growing faster than tendons, more commonly known as the ballerina syndrome, which requires cutting the diet to basics. The general aim is to have youngsters nicely covered without being too fat.

Brood-mares that have been broken in will be easier to produce as they already have a full gearbox and should move better from behind. Lungeing and long-reining in tack (watch out for the foal getting entangled) will help to tone up

Fig 76   *Toccota's Spring Camelia, Rotherwood Foal Champion 1989, shown by the author.*

the lazy or unbroken mares who should be bandaged or booted and in no way be put under any stress when worked. Another method is simply to lead the mare in straight lines in her show tack (which should preferably be a double or pelham bridle and not a snaffle or in-hand bridle) practising a show, walking and trotting as you would in a show ring.

A lot of foals these days look too well handled and too foot perfect, which makes one wonder if they have been worked in tack. It is also these tame foals that become too familiar with the handlers. How often do we see colt foals climbing on nervous female handlers in the show ring, which is extremely dangerous and calls for immediate action otherwise it can develop into a habit!

The foals I have been involved with have just been halter broken at a few days old and lead at walk and trot when going in and out of the fields alongside the mares and everything else has fitted into place over a period of time. Leather foal slips are best as they break if caught on anything and it pays to keep a check on the size as the foal grows.

It will be necessary at the beginning to guide the foal by enveloping him, by putting your left arm around his chest, holding on to the foal slip and your right arm around his quarters. The idea is that the right arm gently encourages the foal forward, preventing him from going backwards and the left arm prevents him from shooting off. Gradually, it will only be necessary to encourage him forward with the right arm when he stops dead in his tracks.

Jerome Harforth leads his foals on the offside of the mare so that the handler is between them both: not only does this make the foal independent and better to lead, it is also easier than when the foal is pulling away from the handler towards mum (which can happen when leading from the nearside).

I make no deliberate attempt to practise a show with foals at home or overhandle them, as I believe this gives them extra presence. The foals that go like clockwork often follow along without sparkle or personality. A knowledgeable judge, having assessed the foal's conformation and seen it walk away and trot for a few strides, should be able to come to a decision and some judges fall for the spontaneity of a cheeky foal.

Foals should be used to having their legs touched and feet picked up at an early age, just in case judges wish to inspect them more closely at a later date. This is also important for the farrier's benefit or in case of emergencies when bathing wounds and so on. If foals can also become accustomed to clippers, rugs, rollers and grooming, it will be a great help in the future and better than having fights when they are much bigger and stronger.

When showing in hand, allow the handler to complement the youngster, just as one does with the rider and horse. For instance, if a foal is rather small, a very tall handler will make the animal look even smaller, just as a large jockey may cover up a dainty, pretty-looking hack and spoil the picture.

If a mare and foal have been turned away after their showing stint, a useful tip is to make sure that the foal is accustomed to corn again before being weaned.

The fashion these days is to have colts cut as yearlings either in the spring or the autumn of that year. Foals are only cut if they really are a handful. If a yearling is very backward, owners leave them a bit longer still. Keeping a yearling entire can give him that extra edge over a yearling gelding in the show ring. This is the very reason that I am not altogether in agreement with colts being shown in the same class as fillies and geldings, which some shows are encouraging.

Initial Schooling for Youngsters

When teaching a youngster to lead in hand, he must learn to walk freely forward alongside the handler, not dragging him or following on behind in the handler's shadow. If the youngster is hanging back, you can either employ the help of an assistant to chase him on from behind or, alternatively, with a long stick in your left hand, tap him on the quarters. The handler must always look ahead; looking at the animal will encourage him to stop in his tracks and retreat. At any stage, animals must be made to think in a forward manner. The same method applies when you teach him to trot. Horses soon learn to copy your stride so the handler must stride on also. If the handler gets left behind, the animal will get his head and be away, apart from the fact that you may be kicked in the process.

The next lesson is to teach the horse to stand quietly, so that he learns to stand correctly and in balance; if foals are taught a little at this stage, it will pay dividends later on.

In general, yearlings should not be lunged unless they are exuberant colts and, then, not in tack, although if the youngster is leaning in, it is a good idea to put a side rein on the outside to correct this. Instead, it is much better to produce them naturally by walking them up and down hills, which many professional yards advocate. Some yearlings need to be bitted with a rubber bit, which must be comfortable in the mouth, being neither too low nor too high and not putting any undue pressure on the mouth. If the animal tends to pull, and leading from the noseband is insufficient, put the coupling (from the bits) on the noseband as well to take away some of the pressure, rather than put direct force on the bits.

When putting a bit and bridle on for the first time, it may be better to put the bridle part on first, with the bit attached to the offside cheekpiece; then put the bit slowly in the mouth, by opening it with your fingers, and attach it to the nearside cheekpiece. This is much better than discovering that the bridle needs adjusting halfway through the exercise, or struggling to put the bridle over the ears because the youngster is wary of the bit in his mouth.

Even though, at the back of your mind, you should still remember that these are youngsters, which are still developing, it doesn't do any harm in your production to look upon three-year-olds as the saddle animal in the making. Some exhibitors even show them in snaffle bridles and, in the hunter classes, double bridles to present this very picture.

Whatever type of bridle you choose to show your mare and youngster in, make sure that it fits. So many have nosebands hanging down and browbands very tight which make their heads look horrendous.

Many people turn two-year-olds away as they are often going through a growing stage, some coming back as much improved while others finish even plainer than they were to begin with. Many experienced breeders believe that good foals return to become good animals at maturity and that you have a fair idea of what you have bred just before the foal dries off after being born.

If showing a two-year-old, you have to decide if you are going to continue producing the animal as you did at yearling stage, but this time with a bit, or whether you are going to educate him more as you would a three-year-old – in tack. Three-year-olds are my favourite and your work preparing them for in hand showing can become the first stages of breaking so that towards the end of the year, they can be backed quite successfully. If you have not already done so, your three-year-old can be mouthed and introduced to lungeing and long-reining.

Long-Reining

Long-reining is very good for youngsters, particularly big young horses because it teaches them to go forward from behind, encouraging them on the bit. Because they are mostly going in straight

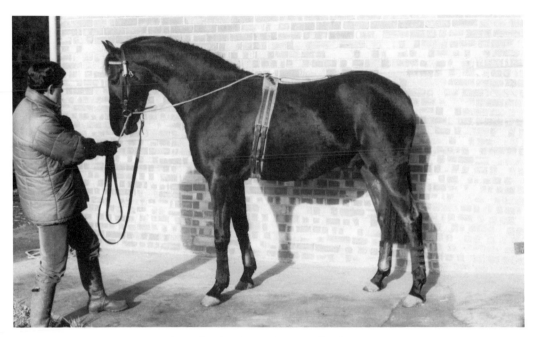

Fig 77 Walking youngsters in tack. An alternative to a fixed
rein: a hand-held running rein just in case a youngster panics in
the early stages. It can be adjusted to suit the individual.

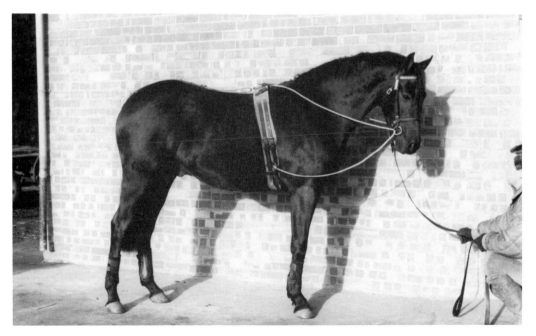

Fig 78 Another alternative to fixed side-reins: a moving cord
system. In this picture, a lower head carriage is encouraged.

Fig 79   Long-reining around the farm, teaching the youngster
to go forward from behind.

Fig 80   Lungeing on the right rein, the right hand is in
control of the head and the left hand ready to encourage the hind
end with the lunge whip (the right hand is acting as the hands;
the left hand is acting as the legs). Note the lunge line is neither
slack nor tense. Also note the protective boots.

lines, as opposed to continuous circling which lungeing entails, it puts less strain on their joints and is a natural progression from teaching the youngster to lead out in hand. However, this is more difficult than lungeing — so must be mastered before being attempted with youngsters, especially at trot. Experts around the country run two-day courses which is certainly something to consider if you feel you are not up to standard.

The trainer must have light, sensitive hands, especially with youngsters, as the control is usually directly on the horse's mouth, whereas with lungeing, the rein is usually attached to the cavesson. It is advisable to wear gloves when both lungeing and long-reining.

A leading show rider once said to me that long-reining is a great art, which he has never attempted to master for two reasons: firstly, he prefers to work from on top, hoping to have horses that are made by God to ride not drive; and, secondly, he doesn't like walking!

Lungeing

Most people prefer lungeing to long-reining as it is within their capabilities. When lungeing youngsters, use your discretion as to how much should be done. Executed well, it can help to tone up the shape as well as help to establish balance, rhythm and improve movement and suppleness. However, many times we see horrific sights on show fields where animals are chased round on the lunge at break neck speed without any leg protection, putting undue strain on joints. Many in hand horses become very one-sided, so lungeing on the stiffer rein can work wonders.

As with long-reining for the first time,

it may be necessary to have an assistant on hand when first lungeing otherwise you may have a horse stopping, starting, shooting off, turning in and spinning in, which should all be discouraged. It would be advisable to lunge with just a cavesson on to begin with, and introduce tack such as a bridle, roller and side-reins at a later stage. A word of warning about side-reins; if put on too tight, they make the animal go behind the movement with the result that he will go in two halves, with extravagant action in front and nothing behind, caused by a stiff back. They should be introduced gradually, just taking the contact to begin with and then used to guide an animal either in a straight line or on a correct bend or to lower or heighten the head carriage. They must never be used as a means of force and are better if they have some elastic in them to simulate the give and take of the sympathetic hand rather than producing a dead effect on the mouth.

The cavesson should be lightweight and well fitting, neither hanging on the head, dropping over the nostrils and in the eyes, nor so tight that the animal can hardly breathe. The lunge rein should be long enough, attached to the middle ring, making sure that the clip doesn't clank on the cavesson ring too much as this can frighten or annoy a youngster.

With the lunge whip and excess loops of lunge rein in your left hand, lead the animal as normal on the left rein in a big circle, gradually leaving the horses side. Then halt him, walking away from him further. On a leftward circle, you will be holding the rein in the left hand (with excess loops in the right) and the whip in the right hand, so that your arms form a 'V' shape; the left hand will be in control of the head and the right hand ready to encourage the hind end with the lunge whip. Ask him to walk on, perhaps flicking the whip at the hindquarters, encouraging him to walk around you, even if this means your keeping on line with the hind legs to begin with. As he becomes accustomed to the idea, gradually make the circle larger, returning to a middle point position behind the horse's shoulders if all goes well.

At first, the lunger will need to do a lot of walking, often keeping close to the hind end to chase him forwards and to remain unyielding. If everything does not go smoothly, get an assistant to lead the horse in a circle with you in the middle giving the commands.

Only when the horse is working well at walk can trot begin, when the handler will have to have his wits about him more. However, it is perhaps better to teach the animal to halt first of all by using your voice, saying 'Halt' or 'Whoa'. If this does not work, give a gentle tug on the lunge rein and, failing that, put the horse into an unjumpable hedge to make him respond. When training a horse on the lunge, the following points should be kept in mind:

1. Use your voice on a one-to-one basis: do not confuse him by having a conversation with a third person.
2. If the horse pulls out, go with him some of the way so that he has nothing to pull against. The lunge rein should be taut, not slack nor about to snap with the tension.
3. Smaller circles make the horse work harder.
4. If the horse tries to escape, work in a confined area.
5. Horses are one-sided so work more on the hard rein.

6. It is better to achieve fifteen minutes good work and stop on a good note.
7. If an animal suddenly stops and falls in, it is because he is going behind the movement. Use your whip more effectively.
8. If he falls in on the lunge, your circle may be too small. Use your whip to push the shoulder out.
9. If he leans out, use your whip to push the quarters out.
10. Only canter on the lunge when the animal is absolutely balanced at walk and trot.

At the Show

Presuming your in-hand star has been trained properly at home, you are now in a position to consider going to a show. On the showground, each animal is different: some can come straight off the horse-box or out of a stable into the ring, whereas others need a walk round either in a headcollar or in tack (some over-exuberant colts may even need a quick lunge). Whatever you do, the ultimate aim is the same: to have a relaxed animal full of presence who is going to give a good account of himself. Unlike the ridden ponies or hacks, who must not show any signs of being over the top in the manners department, youngstock can get away with a little more, although if a judge feels unable to assess fully youngsters because of unruly behaviour, they will be put down the line. Consequently, it does seem sensible to make sure that everything is spot on, especially since there is so little to do compared with, say the ridden hunter or hack.

Although many ridden people think that the in hand job is easy, I can assure you that to be able to perfect an in hand show is just as demanding as the ridden one. There is a considerable art in showing in hand. Often you are dealing with an immature animal who can explode for the simplest of reasons because he has not seen as much as the older animal and, of course, there is no way you can work an in hand animal as hard as you would a ridden hunter, for instance.

With brood-mares, one of the most important considerations is where you are going to put the foal; is he going to follow behind the mare on the outside, which could make the mare hang back, or is he going to walk in front so that she can see him (although often the problem here is that the mare has a longer stride than the foal). This also applies when the mare does her initial trot in front of the judge: do you keep the foal with her, or in the middle of the ring so that she is looking for him or at the other side of the ring so that she will meet him when trotting past the judge. This is when you have to know your animal and how she will react, and it should be remembered that it may be different to the reaction at home because some mares, especially maiden ones, become very foal proud in strange surroundings.

This is also where team work comes into its own. The foal handler must be able to assess when to take the foal away from the mare without upsetting her, which could result in her behaving like a whirling dervish in the initial trot out. In line, the foals normally stand behind the mares, but the fashion these days is to bring the foals to the front to give the mares some interest when the judge looks at each one. This can also apply when the mare comes out of line to stand in front of the judge prior to the individual show.

In line, the handler should have kept his exhibit attentive so that he does not come out of line looking disinterested but leaves at a brisk, businesslike walk. The handler should also have worked out the best possible place to stand his pony up, something which was very important a few years ago at the Royal when most of Ring A was like a quagmire. Never stand an animal downhill, always on the flat or slightly uphill and, if possible, in the direction you intend to walk away, giving you more chance of finding a straight line and avoiding any unnecessary tight turns, which can often lead to animals catching themselves (especially youngsters) and consequently going unlevel.

On the last few strides, try to make sure that the feet are going to finish up in exactly the right position. A judge does not have all day for you to be fiddling about, pulling forwards and pushing backwards for two or three minutes. If the animal does not halt exactly right, know in your own mind whether the animal is better for pushing back a stride or coming forward a stride, to avoid making an even bigger mess.

The judge should be able to see four legs, not two, preferably from the nearside, with the near fore a couple of inches in front of the off fore and the near hind a couple of inches behind the off hind, so that the general picture is one of scope, showing a good length of shoulder and good room from the hip to the hock, ('from the pins to the plate'). If your animal is a little bit long, try not to make the picture even longer by having the animal spread out. Likewise if the animal is very short-coupled and over at the knee, try and stretch him out a little bit, so that he does not look like a card table with collapsible legs, all bunched together.

Fig 81   A well-turned-out jockey standing her 14.2hh pony correctly for the judge Mrs Renita White.

This is why it is a great help if you know your horse's weak points, so that you can try to produce around them. It is amazing that breeders are able to find faults with other people's stock but cannot see faults in their own.

As soon as the animal is standing, either with a piece of grass or paper or by making a noise with your stick by tapping the number on your back, attempt to make the horse look interested. A show animal looking disinterested is a pitiful sight. Common mistakes at this point are standing alongside the pony so that the judge cannot see the pony fully, or startling the animal by throwing grass in the air which makes it move backwards into a heap.

Some animals look better with their head carriage lower and longer, which can be positioned at this stage, others look better nicely arched. Bad presentation is, when in order to give a pony an elevated long front, the ignorant handler has the head so high that the muscle underneath the neck is very prominent, which does nothing for the appearance of the overall topline.

When the judge moves to the front do not get in his way and make sure your animal is standing square from both the front and behind: when the judge moves to the other side, move your animal either one stride forwards or backwards. If there are two judges looking from both sides, make sure that you are not standing your pony up for the probationary judge by mistake!

Depending on how the mare has behaved, the foal can either go with the mare in the show, providing he does not get in the way of the judge's vision or, better still, be led in the opposite direction to the mare, so that she will meet him when trotting past the line. This should have been discussed beforehand as it always pays to plan a strategy.

Walk the mare away from the judge in a straight line (if you have planned it carefully, you will be on a good piece of ground), focusing on something at the side of the ring to help keep the line. Keep the strides long and even. Unless the judge has specified otherwise, walk away

Fig 82   A competitor walking away from the in hand judge, Arthur Illsley, in a straight line during the conformation stage at the Horse of the Year Show. If a show animal is not 100 per cent level, it will be revealed more on the concrete surface than the more cushioned going of a grass main ring.

for as long as you dare, especially if your mare is a straight mover, so that the judge will have that extra bit of time to see you trot back, and also to allow you to rectify anything that might go wrong, like breaking into canter.

Turn off your track left, then turn her neatly back on to the same track with you on the outside circle; if you turn the mare around yourself, she will probably step on your toes, apart from the fact it is incorrect to do so for this reason. Wait until you are on a straight line, then start to trot at a nice balanced pace; if you trot on the turn she will become unbalanced and probably catch herself — apart from the fact that brood-mares do not want to be turned on a sixpence. If you do not bother to turn off the track at walk but just turn, this means the judge has to walk a couple of yards to find your line, which is bad manners. Some misguided people try to disguise the fact their animals do not move straight by not trotting directly towards the judge; in most cases, this is in vain as any judge worth his salt will request a second run. Once past the judge, you can open the mare out a bit more, so that the judge can catch a glimpse as you go around the back of the line which, you hope, will make a lasting impression.

Always be on the ball when in line, as the judges often cast a glance at the line up while looking at other exhibits. If your mare is half asleep and looks nothing, this could be enough to loose your placing. Be ready to walk off smartly for the final walk round; this is often the critical stage and even though some judges have made their minds up by now, others may still be pondering. At this stage your mare may have been in the ring for over an hour, in hot weather, so you have to pull out all the stops to create that final good impression. I have seen some exhibitors, in order to wake up their flagging mare, run their showing cane along the railings at the side of the ring, or go near the edge of the ring, hoping that the buzzing from the spectators will help.

Remember, even when back in line, the class is not over until the rosettes are handed out; some judges who are still undecided swap placings around again. It is usually at this stage we observe which exhibitors are aware of the qualification proceedings and have all the correct membership cards for all the special rosettes on offer, like the NPS medal rosette, etc.

When the mare class is finished, judges sometimes ask for foals to come forward. Some of them are quite independent and can do an individual performance without mum's help, whereas others not as confident need the mare alongside throughout the show. You have to be ready for either situation.

When trotting foals, either towards the judge in the show or as a class, it pays to keep them at a steadier pace than older animals because they are more likely to break into canter or stop dead if pushed too much or, alternatively, not enough. Foals definitely need a little more sympathetic handling and can make fools of you so easily if you bully or confuse them.

Tyranny and cruelty will more speedily in the horse than ever in the child, provoke the wish to disobey and, on every practicable occasion, the resistance to command. The restive and vicious horse is in ninety nine cases out of a hundred, made so by ill-usage and not by nature.

Make sure you have a long enough lead rein so that if the foal should pull away from you sharply, you can give him some extra line so that he will have nothing to pull against, so lessening the risk of his panicking. However, do not give him too much or, as when lungeing, you may be dragged.

Compared to brood-mares, which are older and have probably been ridden and are therefore a lot more balanced and less spooky, youngstock are more unpredictable in the ring and demand extra concentration.

We can split youngstock into two main categories: there is the very forward-thinking animal or the hanging back, timid type and depending which you have, you should use the rest of the class accordingly and to your advantage.

With the former type, it may be better to lead the class in so that he looks interested but at the same time is aware of others behind him, which makes him think about coming back into his bridle (almost like a half-halt). If you manage to keep this lead on the initial trot round, it should work well, in that to begin with, the pony will remain collected and then open up just at the right time when he sees the end of the queue at the other side of the ring.

It is far better to walk a few strides before trotting in order to keep the pony's balance; then, when in trot, keep the pony up to his bridle to achieve this balance and activity from behind, gradually allowing more head as the pony floats into a slightly longer stride without running and remember to keep the pony's head straight and not facing in towards you which gives the impression of the animal being short of front and going bridle lame. Use your showing cane to keep the pony from falling in on you and turning his head towards you.

Some people also thread the rein from the nearside ring through the outside ring to counteract this. Try also to come down to walk just as accurately – do not go crashing into the rest of the animals like a runaway train.

If you do not manage to keep your lead and are not first to trot, it may pay to turn the pony's head away and let him look at the pony behind when the one in front of you sets off, otherwise he may panic and want to follow, so that when it is your turn, he sets off like a greyhound in a trap.

For the backward-thinking youngster, get tucked in behind the one in front for a lead and do the opposite to that described above for the forward-thinking youngster when the one in front starts his initial trot so that yours is eager to leave his friends behind. (Also, do not go too close to the one behind you.) Similarly, when standing out for your individual show, keep the nappy one further away from the line-up, so that he does not hang back to the others. When in the line-up, be careful not to stand too close to animals either side of you, particularly in a mixed class like a Championship when it is possible to have mares and stallions at close proximity.

Always teach your in hand prospect from a foal upwards to stand settled in line. You will be frowned upon by judges, stewards and fellow exhibitors alike if your youngster disrupts the line-up – all it needs is one unruly animal and it escalates down the line like a pack of cards and the judge may have no option but to send you out, if he considers you to be a danger to the others. A colleague used to have trouble in line with her yearling colt who 'would not stand still for one minute as he had a very active mind and was always up to mischief'. She used to take an aniseed rag in the ring with her to keep him occupied, which seemed to do the trick.

Unless your steward wishes you to go into a Championship in class order, try and go behind a foal to give your youngster a bit more lift and presence, especially if he is flagging by the time the Championship is due.

Many other tips concerning in hand showmanship are also given in Chapter 7 on ringcraft. If ever in doubt what to do, just watch the handful of experts who have perfected this art and who present their animals in a very quiet, slick manner time and time again as opposed to the people whose animals are too fit, badly bridled and always get loose in the ring because the handlers have no control whatsoever. Experts such as Len Bigley and Colin Rose always seem to have their animals beautifully balanced and very interested.

Fig 83 Lechlade Quince, a quality 12.2 hh riding pony yearling, well presented by Colin Rose to win at the Great Yorkshire Show. (Co-owned by the author.)

Fig 84   Measuring a riding pony yearling at Shropshire and West Midlands Show.

Youngstock in certain sections are subject to measuring on the showground, so it is common sense to make sure that they are accustomed to strangers with measuring sticks or you could have trouble getting the animal measured in especially if he is uptight and on his toes. The best type of measuring pads at shows are those in a stable; the worst ones are those which are just a concrete slab at the edge of the ring – often you can have a job making the youngster walk on to it, let alone stand!

Measuring is sometimes done before the classes start but, at other times, during the class. In theory, the former method could be open to abuse and there is no way the vets will know for sure if the animal they measure in the morning is the one that will be competing in the ring, as

there are no means of checking identity. (At least with height certificates for the older animal, there is a means of checking identification.) Measuring during the class would eliminate this situation, if it ever arose, but can be time consuming. Often the classes are delayed while the end of the line-up is still outside the ring being measured. I am surprised that they do not measure these while the judge is concentrating on the top ones and vice versa.

I feel sorry for those exhibitors whose youngsters measure quite easily at the beginning of the season and then grow rapidly, so that they have to go into the next height section, often being at a disadvantage as they are giving away a lot of height, or worse still do not have another class to go into at all (as is the case with the 14.2hh pony). This must be galling, when a lot of money has been paid in wasted entry fees and especially when at the end of the day the animal will still measure within the height limit at maturity for ridden classes.

Even though a further half inch is allowed after 1st July for all height categories in youngstock classes, it is thought by many that this still does not give enough scope to, say, the larger three-year-old bracket; it is commonly felt that most 12.2hh youngsters do most of their growing early on and often do not grow much more after two years of age while, on the other hand, the 14.2hh continues to grow. Yet they are both subjected to the same height margins.

If you do have a youngster who is very close to his height limit, this is yet another reason for working very closely with your farrier. A good blacksmith, like a good vet, is an important asset to any showing yard at any time, and can work with great effect on youngstock when there are problems.

Judging an In Hand Class

When judging an in hand class, it is very important to refer to the wording of the schedule and, if it states hunter pony breeding, bear that in mind. I remember an incident when my mare Pendle Atalanta, who was really a small riding horse rather than a small hunter (even though she won shows like the Great Yorkshire, beating horses like Sporting Print and Crown of Crowns which were model small hunters), won a Supreme Broodmare Championship at a good breeding show one year. The year after, obviously

full of high hopes and great expectations of repeating this success, we finished only second in the class to a mare that was giving away a lot of height, under Babs Ruchwaldy who thought a lot of my mare. She said, quite rightly, that she felt happier that the winning mare could fulfil the wording of the schedule, which had been altered from light horse breeding the year before to large pony breeding.

When I did my probationary judging, I was told that if I ever suspected a youngster to be overheight for the category (and there were no facilities for measuring at the show), I should reassess the situation immediately.

In mixed classes, it is very important to ask the ages of the animals; often two-year-olds look like three-year-olds and unless you discover this, you could give a two-year-old the Championship thinking it was a three-year-old.

When I judge youngstock, I look for saddle potential apart from good conformation, movement and presentation. I consequently assess conformation as something which is pleasing to the eye and not as a measurement exercise where you measure the head to see if it measures the same as from the hock to the ground, and so on. I would rather have a youngster with an abundance of quality and presence, who may be slightly less correct than something that is almost near perfection (nothing is perfect), but lacks star quality.

I always like my youngsters to stand over the ground well and have good movement. They will have a better future than the ultra short-coupled ones that cannot get out of their own stride. Yearlings who have scope are often leggy, which at this stage is acceptable, whereas two-year-olds should be maturing away from this by then. Three-year-olds should at least look like potential saddle animals and if you cannot see where the saddle is going to be, then there is something wrong. Some faults, like being weak behind may be acceptable in a yearling, but not at a later stage when you would expect it to have improved. Similarly, being higher behind than in front is acceptable in young stock since they grow in different stages, but it is not acceptable in the older animal.

Perhaps the most difficult classes to judge are the foal classes, because they can make a fool of a judge, especially if he has his winning foal near the bottom a few weeks later at another show; this is not a sign of inconsistency, but demonstrates how foals can change rapidly in a short space of time.

I like to see a foal that is in proportion and has a good sloping shoulder, stands square and is a straight balanced mover. I always like to ask how many weeks old each foal is, to bring them down to a common denominator. If I cannot decide about two foals and both are at opposite ends of the line-up, which makes it difficult to compare, I will often put them next to each other for a closer look. As with most judging, it is often the one that catches your eye on the day that wins.

Fig 85 Whalton Ragtime (13.2hh), Champion Pony at RIHS in 1967. She won the Lloyds Bank In Hand Championship six years later, the only pony brood-mare to date to achieve this.

98

Fig 86   Ainsty Merry Maid with the author after winning the Supreme Championship at Lincoln Show in 1988. A grand-daughter of Lloyds Champion, Whalton Ragtime, she was Reserve to Hunting Eve for the Judy Creber title in 1989.

When judging brood-mares, I like them to look like brood-mares, within reason, not just saddle animals that have a foal (although novice mares can sometimes get away with this a bit more) nor something which waddles about the ring very heavy in foal. A good show brood-mare should be correct and have substance and quality. She should not be a weed nor, on the other hand, should she be big and plain (what has been described by some as a paddock mare).

I was fortunate to have been involved with the 12.2hh brood-mare Ainsty Merry Maid who won the pony in hand section at Wembley in 1989. What made her particularly exceptional for her category was that judges could see that she

would still have been appealing at 16.2hh, whereas many other smaller mares would have become weedier for being much bigger; this appeal is the essence of a top-class pony brood-mare.

Some judges like to see stallions very masculine. However, I sometimes wonder if this is not mistaken for plainness instead. In my opinion, the ideal stallion should be handsome rather than pretty and should be correct and full of quality both in build and action.

There are too many bad colts kept on for breeding these days which is a very dangerous situation because, while bad mares can only breed one foal per year, a bad stallion is capable of a lot more damage in a season.

There are so many opportunities for in hand exhibitors these days, particularly in the pony classes with so many different Championships to qualify for and in which most people seem to participate, that it has reached a point where everyone is qualifying mad. Anything which encourages showing is good, providing it does not encourage people to over-show. Although a points scheme provides another alternative to normal competition, some people are now wondering if these are won by the people who are prepared to travel the most, rather than by the best animals. Consequently, societies are looking at further alternatives to discourage this.

Championship Shows

Of the Sunrise, Glyn Greenwood, Colbeach, D. J. Riseley and JCB competitions, the most interesting is the in hand final at Wembley which is still as prestigious today as it was twenty-five years ago, giving the breeder more recognition and putting him on the same level as the ridden exhibitors.

The first in hand Championship at Wembley started in 1965, when it was sponsored by Fredericks and Pelhams Timber Buildings, the loose box manufacturers, and was called the Fredericks Champion of the Year. It was modest compared to the modern-day one, but the object was the same: to find the supreme light horse or pony in hand Champion of the year, irrespective of type or breed (excluding heavy horse breeds), and working on a similar basis to the Supreme Champion at Crufts and the Smithfield Show.

From the beginning, it evoked a great deal of criticism and controversy, as many claimed that it would be impossible to ask any judge to select the best in hand exhibit from a line-up with such diverse types as, for example, a Welsh Mountain pony, a Shetland pony, a young hunter and an Arab brood-mare. One school of thought was that in future years there may be a tendency for judges to feel that they ought to give the ponies a chance one year, as the hunters had perhaps dominated the class the previous year. However, even as the first winner completed his lap of honour in the London spotlight, few people could disagree that the event was a great success, creating a new interest in breed classes and earning a rightful place amongst the other Wembley competitions, a thought which still exists today, some twenty-five years later.

In the first year, there were nine qualifying events: the Newark and Nottingham County Show, the Oxford County Show, the Bath and West Show, the Richmond Royal Horse Show, the Three Counties Show, the Northumberland County Show, the Kent County Show, Royal Welsh Show and the Ponies of Britain Summer Show, and the winners of each event went to Wembley to compete for a £100 cash prize and a trophy.

The most interesting aspect of the competition was the wide variety of breeds that competed against each other, both at the qualifying shows and the final. The line-up at Wembley was as follows:

1. The Arab brood-mare Gold Royal owned by Lady Blunt, who qualified at Richmond.
2. Coed Coch Pelydrog, a Welsh Sec-

tion A, owned by Lt. Col. E. W. Williams-Wynn, who qualified at the Royal Welsh.

3. Mr J. G. Henson's hunter The Truth, who qualified at Oxford.

4. The former ridden Pony of the Year 1959/60, Arden Tittle Tattle, who qualified at Newark for Mrs Joy Hillman and who finished second in the final.

5. One of two hunter brood-mares, Pleasant Fancy, who qualified at Bath and West and finished third at Wembley in the ownership of Lt. Col. and Mrs. Ivor Reeves.

6. Vean Zaffer, a Dartmoor stallion owned by Mrs. W. E. Robinson, qualifying at Kent County.

7. Penny Farthing, a three-year-old rangey, chasing type hunter gelding by Pendragon, owned by Mrs Molly Cail, and qualifying at Northumberland.

8. The second Welsh Section A, also owned by Lt. Col. Williams-Wynn, Coed Coch Anwyled who triumphed at the Ponies of Britain.

9. The eventual winner of the Fredericks Championship, Mrs A. L. Woods' Prince's Grace, an eleven-year-old bay hunter mare who qualified at the Three Counties Show, bred by Rex Chappell by Prince's Game, ex Collence.

Critics need not have worried about any imbalance as two hunter brood-mares finished first and third, and three ponies second, fourth and fifth.

The following year, the Royal Highland Show also became a qualifier and appropriately enough sent a Highland pony to the final, a four-year-old stallion called Glentromie Trooper, who eventually finished second. Of the other nine finalists, Prince's Grace qualified yet again at

the Malvern showground on her first outing of the season and Mrs Cail once again qualified a three-year-old hunter called Winning Coin at Northumberland County. Another Section A bearing the Coed Coch prefix, this time Siglen Las, beat the Shetland Leapyatt Nelson, to qualify at Oxford for owner Miss R. Russell.

Arabs seemed to be more in abundance than in later years and these included a seven-year-old stallion, El Meluk by Minkeno, owned by Mrs Linney and qualifying at Newark; the Crabbet bred and owned Nerinora, who qualified at Richmond; and Mrs Robert Crawford's two-year-old Anglo Arab colt Carbrook Surprise who beat not only the hunter Nell Gwynne at Kent County to qualify, but also won the final judged by Mrs Pennell and Mr J. G. Henson. Others forward included Elspeth Ferguson's legendary eight-year-old Bwlch Zephyr who qualified at the last possible chance at Ponies of Britain and finished third; the homebred two-year-old filly by Rouge Croix, ex Question, Mr and Mrs Norman Skinner's Bath and West winner, Criss Cross; and finally, Mr Emrys Griffiths' section A brood-mare Clan Peggy who, not surprisingly, qualified at the Royal Welsh Show.

In 1967, Class 11 in the schedule was judged by Mr E. G. E. Griffiths and Mr B. Cleminson and the catalogued entries read as follows:

336 Brockwell Cobweb, chestnut roan stallion, eight years.
Sire: Harford Starlight (1825).
Dam: Fayre Ladybird (FS2 1880).
Exhibitor: Mrs B. K. Binnie, Brockwell Farm, Wootten Courtenay, Minehead, Somerset.

337 Christmas Carol of Bennochy, bay colt, one year.
Sire: Lennel Strolling Minstrel.
Dam: Swift.
Breeder: Her Grace the Duchess of Roxburghe.
Exhibitor: Miss M. E. Macharg, Woodside Stud Kelso.

338 Crown Turton, liver-chestnut gelding, three years.
Sire: Turton Fair (GSB).
Dam: Coronette II.
Breeder: Mr D. Westwood.
Exhibitors: Mr and Mrs W. J. C. Thomas, Lodge Farm, Great Billing, Northants.

339 Gredington Simwnt (WSB 3614), grey stallion, 11.2hh, six years.
Sire: Coed Coch Madog (1981).
Dam: Coed Coch Symwl (9509).
Exhibitor: The Right Hon. Lord Kenyon, Gredington, Whitchurch, Salop.

340 Honyton Michael Ap Briant (4103), palomino stallion, five years.
Exhibitor: M. Isaac, Ty'r Capel Stud, Penrhiwgyngi, Manmoel, Blackwood, Mon.

341 Kilbees High Jinks (PBDR 61 Vol. 1) chestnut colt, one year.
Sire: Kilbees Gay Jenkin.
Dam: Kilbees Royal Return (PBAR Vol. 5).
Breeder: The Marchioness of Willingdon.
Exhibitor: The Marchioness of Willingdon, Kilbees Farm, Winkfield Windsor, Berks.

342 Micawber (AASB, NPSB) chestnut gelding, 15hh, two years.
Sire: Mikeno.
Dam: Irish Luck.
Breeder: Maj. M. V. Argyle MC, QC.

Exhibitor: Mrs. R. A. Mallender, Elmfield, Horning, Norwich, Norfolk.

343 Nell Gwynne, brown filly, three years.
Sire: Regent.
Dam: Becky Jones.
Breeder: J. L. Burgess.
Exhibitor: J. L. Burgess, Wooton Manor Farm, Polegate, Sussex.

344 Rosevean Ripple (RPR Vol 36) chestnut mare, 14.1hh, five years.
Sire: Bwlch Zephyr.
Dam: Tidcombe Maple.
Breeder: Miss S. E. Ferguson.
Exhibitor: Miss J. Pettigrew, Park Farm, Newton Hall Lane, Mobberley, Knutsford, Cheshire.

345 Tom Jones, chestnut, three years.
Sire: Kadir Cup.
Exhibitor: Miss M. L. Steavenson, Stapleton Manor, Stapleton, Darlington, Co. Durham.

In this class, Mostyn Isaac's Hoynton Michael Ap Braint came first; Crown Turton came second; Nell Gwynne came third and Micawber came fourth. Interestingly enough, the winner returned to Wembley twenty-two years later as a personality, the very same year that one of his grandsons Penclose Welsh Monarch qualified for the same competition, shown by Mostyn Isaac's son Elvide.

Each Wembley Champion is an equine star, but the first superstar to emerge from this in hand Championship was the winner for the next two years, Col. Rosser John's Treharne Tomboy shown by David Reynolds. In 1968, Tomboy qualified at Three Counties and headed a line-up which included four hunters; Highyield (3rd), Parlez Vous (2nd), Bondsman and Harbour Rock; another

Section A, Kidwell Pipson; a Welsh Cob, Lyn Cwmcoed; a Highland, Glenmuick; and a riding pony, Petula. The following year, Tomboy beat Oakley Bubbling Spring and Parlez Vous in that order. Unfortunately, he became the last of the Frederick's Champions as the competition folded and did not return to the Wembley Arena again until 1972, when it was renamed the Lloyds In Hand Championship.

At the instigation of Lord Kenyon, the owner of the successful Gredington stud of Welsh ponies and one of the directors of Lloyds Bank, this financial institution with the symbol of the black horse (which originated from a sign hung in Lombard Street three hundred years before), firmly established an even greater equine spectacle, which delighted both spectators and breeders alike for a further seventeen years and, most notably, opened up the segregated in hand world even further.

Those people who originally thought that the competition would be biased in favour of either horses or ponies will be interested to know that, at the time of writing, the horses have won the Lloyds final nine times and the ponies eight times.

The superstars of the Lloyds era, equalling Tomboy's record include two ponies and one hunter: Rosevean Eagles Hill, who won as a yearling and as a three-year-old; Llanarth Flying Comet who won in successive years; and Hunting Eve the lovely chestnut mare by Three Wishes, expertly shown on each occasion by John Rawdings. This mare not only won two Lloyds titles but then went on into the record books by winning for the third consecutive year in 1989, when the competition was renamed the Judy Creber In Hand final following the policy decision of Lloyds to pull out. Incidentally, the black horse in the Lloyds Bank television adverts is Jolly Tramp, Donald Owen's lightweight hunter Champion, who also appeared in the Black Beauty series.

In 1972, when Mr Norman Crow's three-year-old hunter Fresco won, there were only seven qualifying rounds. This number was increased over the years to fourteen to give more people who were not prepared to travel long distances an opportunity to take part. There followed a further increase to seventeen, when it was decided to include the three specialist breed shows: the National Pony Show, the National Hunter Show and the Arab Show, thus giving a wider range of opportunities for all our breeds to qualify, as the wording in the catalogue so rightly stated. In 1973 the class was divided into two sections with all the participants placed in the Championship; the year after the class was organized as we see it today.

In 1989, in the Judy Creber Championship, there were still only seventeen qualifiers, which most exhibitors say is sufficient in order to safely accommodate stallions and mares in the limited space of the Wembley arena and if the prestige of the competition is to remain. Also, the task of the judges is difficult enough as it is, without increasing the numbers any further.

Even though comparing animals of different age and breed has always needed an expert eye, many judges enjoy the challenge. Mrs Jennifer Clapham who judged the first Judy Creber final with Mr Willie Goldie, told me that she had never enjoyed herself as much in all her years as a judge. However, it is not only the judges who enjoy the competition but also the enthusiastic exhibitors, whether they choose to set out their stall (entering every qualifying show) or whether they leave it to chance (not wishing to travel extensively and so hoping to be in the right place at the right time). In many ways, their achievement is greater than any of the other Wembley showing exhibitors, because often they have had to go under many different judges to qualify in the first place.

Often, when looking through the schedules at the beginning of the season, if one fancies one's chances under a particular 'Lloyds' judge at, for example, the South of England, the judge of your section is usually not as promising and vice versa – so one is constantly reminded that there is a strong element of luck involved. If you think you may be lucky and become Champion of your section (or even luckier if you are eligible as Reserve because your vanquisher has already qualified), the situation is very similar to section competing at the BSPS Championships, in that you will be faced with a dilemma: do you have your animal sharp at the beginning of the day, thereby risking all, but then still have some petrol in the tank just in case you get through to the qualifying round at the end of the day or following day? Or, alternatively, do you have your animal spot on for the preliminary classes and hope a change of ring (often the qualifying rounds are judged in the main ring for maximum publicity) will be enough to give your tired animal an extra boost?

At some shows, judges are allowed a preliminary look at the animals forward prior to the final judging in the main ring. I judged a qualifier at Essex Show some years ago and was told not to give the result away by obviously spending more time with a selected few. Of course I obeyed this to the letter, to the point that the ones I did not like, I appeared to spend slightly longer with, so that in the collecting ring, unbeknown to me, exhibitors who had no chance were convinced otherwise. Even though these people were soon to be disappointed, the outcome was just as exciting as the eventual winner and reserve were equally surprised and delighted.

I felt that it was very important to know what each animal represented and was therefore able to assess whether it was a good Champion or not, apart from the fact that conformation and presentation also played an important part. Some judges even think about what those animals are going to look like at Wembley and often qualify the one that they think will stand the best possible chance when they get there. This is one of the reasons that yearlings very seldom qualify as opposed to the older stock, which have stopped growing and altering.

If you are fortunate enough to qualify for Wembley, then what happens next? Do you continue showing as planned and make Wembley just another show, arriving there with a lot of form and press attention in the hope of influencing the judges, or do you deliberately withdraw your animal from the showing scene so that it arrives there unbeaten since qualifying, as fresh as a daisy? If you opt for the latter, make sure that you give yourself enough time to get your Champion in peak condition again and be careful not to let the winter coat come through.

There are also many other considerations: with a three-year-old, would you consider breaking him to give him some-

Fig 87   Fall Edge Sundance, winner of the Lloyds Bank In Hand final in 1984 and Reserve for the title in 1986.

thing to think about, as his season is now longer than normal, without the risk of his losing flesh or putting any wear on his joints? With a brood-mare, you have the choice of either weaning the foal or leaving him on the mare. From the point of view of producing the latter, it would be far easier to show just the mare and have only one animal to prepare both on and before the day. Another advantage to weaning the foal is that the mare would not be worried about her foal in the strange surroundings of the arena. Also, by the time October comes around, and particularly if he is an early foal, mares are often getting fed up with a large, fit, active foal. On the other hand, the overall picture of a brood-mare may well be lost without a foal at her side especially if she is not in foal again and looks a little light

although if a mare is heavily in foal again she may perform better with a foal as bait and her looks would be accepted as part of the picture with a foal at her side. Most brood-mares compete at Wembley accompanied by foals.

The experienced Wembley in hand exhibitors are well aware of the standards of production required if they are to stand any chance on the day and each year their job is becoming more and more difficult, as people try even harder to have their animals looking 'a million dollars'. In fact, this is echoed throughout the season. Animals that are badly turned out and look dirty, especially greys with long yellow tails, are very noticeable (for the wrong reason!)

To keep an in hand animal fresh and fit looking at that time of year is certainly a

Fig 88   Celtic Ballad, Best Riding Pony Stallion and Lloyds qualifier at the NPS Show in 1985. Seven weeks later, he captured the Wembley title judged by Mrs Joan Gibson and David Nicholson.

demanding job: mares are starting to look bad tempered, stallions may have had a busy covering season and youngstock can alter their shape rapidly. Consequently, they all need constant supervision and attention if they are to remain in peak condition for several weeks longer than normal.

Even though the production standards have risen, the standard of dress of some of the handlers leaves a lot to be desired. The majority do not seem to realize that they are at a top London show and some

look as though they are about to start painting and decorating the spare room. Perhaps the time has come for the show itself to lay down some strict rules, as they do for the other classes. If the judge, the show officials and some of the exhibitors can make the effort, then so should the few that let the side down. To have qualified and competed in either the Fredericks, Lloyds or Judy Creber In Hand final is a great achievement, and it would seem a great pity if you did not look your best in your moment of glory.

Fig 89   Prince's Grace at the National Hunter Show after winning the Brood-mare Championship for the third time. She was the first Fredericks Champion at Wembley in 1965.

PAST WINNERS

Fredericks In Hand Championship

1965   Mrs A. L. Wood's *Prince's Grace* (hunter mare)

1966   Mrs R. Crawford's *Carbrook Surprise* (Anglo Arab two-year-old colt)

1967   M. Isaac's *Honyton Michael Ap Briant* (Welsh Section D)

1968   Col. Rosser John's *Treharne Tomboy* (Welsh Section A)

1969   *Treharne Tomboy* (see 1968)

Lloyds Bank In Hand Championship

1972   Mr Norman Crow's *Fresco* (hunter three-year-old)

1973   Mr and Mrs J. C. Alton's *Whalton Ragtime* (pony mare)

1974   L. S. Ivens' and Mrs P. Jackson's *Sammy Dasher* (hunter three-year-old)

1975   Mrs V. A. Ferguson's *Clipston* (hunter three-year-old)

1976   Miss S. E. Ferguson's *Rosevean Eagles Hill* (pony yearling colt)

*Fig 90 Hunting Eve at the South of England Show in 1987
where she first qualified for the In Hand Championship at
Wembley, a final she won three years in succession.*

1977 Mr and Mrs A. McCowan's *Three Wishes* (hunter three-year-old)
1978 *Rosevean Eagles Hill (see 1976)*
1979 University College of Wales' *Llanarth Flying Comet* (Welsh Section D)
1980 *Llanarth Flying Comet (see 1979)*
1981 Mrs D. Nicholson's *Little Primrose* (hunter mare)
1982 Miss A. Murray's *Mallard Court* (hunter mare)
1983 Mr and Mrs T. W. Irving's *Winneydene Satellite* (Welsh Section A)

1984 Mr and Mrs F. W. Furness' *Falledge Sundance* (pony stallion)
1985 Mrs D. E. M. Alexander's *Celtic Ballad* (light horse stallion)
1986 Mrs M. E. Mansfield's *Chirk Windflower* (three-year-old pony)
1987 Miss A. J. Murray's *Hunting Eve* (hunter mare)
1988 *Hunting Eve (see 1987)*

Judy Creber In Hand Championships

1989 *Hunting Eve (see 1987)*

5 The Working Classes

Probably what makes the working hunter, cob and pony classes so popular, is that there is still an exciting element of chance involved, with performance rather than outstanding beauty a major criterion. From an interest point of view, each class is different from the other, whereas there is nothing to distinguish normal showing classes once the season is underway – established Champions in these very rarely have off-days and remain unbeaten especially in the ridden hunter classes – but fortunes vary a great deal more in the working classes and big winners can soon be brought down to earth by just rolling a pole in a momentary lapse of concentration, thus giving a lesser animal more opportunity of beating a well-known name.

A wider section of people are attracted to these classes each year and from the beginning become completely immersed in the competition, often coming from a hunting and pony club background, and therefore appreciating the performance element of the classes. Because these classes are governed by a marking system (the results sheets of which are open to closer inspection after the classes), there is a greater understanding of judges' preferences, which is also a great attraction. Compare this to the showing exhibitors who take longer to learn the artistry involved and, to this day, cannot understand some of the judges' decisions, which are based purely on personal and private opinion.

Also, not every rider wants a horse who has to be wrapped up in cotton wool, who often has a difficult temperament and is likely to hot up or refuse if asked to do more than light work. Although not all show animals are useless, their working colleagues have many other uses, which is an important consideration with today's increasing costs, and will give riders a great deal more fun without having to worry about blemishes and so on. In other words, he is the good all-rounder with showing potential.

The major part of the competition is the jumping section and, no matter how attractive your animal, if he cannot jump a competent round, he will not succeed in the working competitions. Sixty per cent of the total marks are awarded in the jumping phase in BSPS, HIS and working cob classes. On the whole, courses are no longer thrown together with remnants from the show-jumping ring, but are constructed by experts who do produce a good testing course which provides an interesting spectacle for exhibitors and general public alike.

Very rarely do we see a course that is riding so badly that judges need to abandon the class in the interest of safety although, when it has happened, it has been because the distances between fences have not been altered to accommodate the bigger animals or the course is too difficult for the standard of the competitor, doing little to boost the confidence of the animal.

The job of the course builder is to find the happy balance by knowing the stan-

Fig 91   Walking the course at the BSPS Winter Championships.

dard of competitor involved. Building too easy a course is also pointless and makes the jumping section more or less a mere formality and, surprisingly enough, it is often the Champion or perhaps his jockey who, through having no respect for the size of the fences, falls by the wayside in such a situation.

Walking the Course

At all levels of this type of competition, classes are lost either because the animals are not ready for that level of sport due to lack of schooling at home or because the rider has failed to understand the importance of walking the course. At top level, you can no longer just amble into the ring and fly over the fences; instead, you have to assess and understand the problems that the course builder has set for you; so the first priority when arriving at the show is to examine the course to see what difficulties are in store.

The first consideration is to walk the track you intend to take when riding, establishing a sense of direction. By memorizing the course, even if this means doing it in sections, you can give all your attention to your horse during the jumping round. Use a certain marker such as a tractor or a trade stand outside the ring to help you remember lines through staggered or off-set fences, particularly if you need to take a big sweeping approach into a fence. It pays to look back after a couple of fences when walking the track to double-check on your line, although this should not be done when riding, even if you have tapped or rolled a pole.

Apart from remembering heights and distances, you must locate the danger area where the course builder is testing your ability, particularly if your horse has a special hang-up like bullfinches or leaving the collecting ring entrance. Only by walking the course properly, which means concentrating totally on the job in

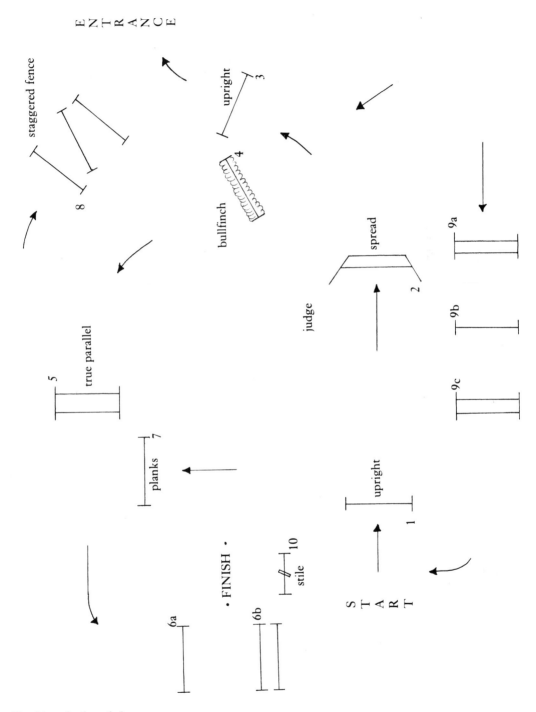

Fig 92   A plan of the course.

hand, will you be able to assess the standard of the course. It may even be too much for your horse, especially if he is a novice, in which case you will have to decide whether to leave him in the box. Like all aspects of showing, knowing your own and your horse's capabilities can pay dividends. Similarly, if you feel out of your depth, it would be advisable to walk the course with someone more experienced.

Assessing the Course

Instead of discussing heights and distance problems, which can become very time consuming, Fig 92 shows a plan of a course that you can meet at any good show with good entries (possibly a qualifier).

Fence 1 is a typical starter and comprises a simple brush fence with a pole, just slightly above minimum height. It is encouraging as it is going towards home and is not too daunting. However, be careful not to approach the fence too casually or you may end up rolling a pole. The first fence is usually where you can rely on setting your animal up with a great deal of accuracy as you have him concentrating without running on, which is necessary in this case as fence 2 is within sight (being in line with number one).

One of the most common sights is an animal becoming more excited as he progresses through the course and, what started as an accurate, stylish round gradually develops into an Evil Knieval display, resulting in horses standing well back from the fences and putting spectators' hearts in their mouths.

Fence 2 is a small spread, also quite straight forward as it is not up to height,

but needs more attack as it is a wide fence with a log wall as a filler. This should not present any problems; in many ways it is much better than if it had been another upright, as you are already on a committed line from fence 1 and the horse has probably spotted it either when approaching fence 1 or while in mid-air. The main problem is not to stand off too much but at the same time being careful not to get into the bottom of the log pile, which would cause a windy animal to stop. The fence itself is inviting especially as the wings are positioned at an angle (enveloping you), rather than straight.

The course builder should not present hazards before the first two or three fences as these are supposed to get the horse and rider off to a good start; often, these fences are inviting and not up to height. The entries at this show must be of a reasonable standard as the first problem fence is 3, an upright situated in a dip, making the approach slightly downhill.

Horses will naturally lengthen their stride going downhill which makes it more difficult to be accurate with the take-off point. Upright fences demand accurate jumping and so your horse needs to be collected, especially after jumping a spread fence. Luckily, the slight turn to the left, although heading into downhill territory, should help you to steady the horse; if the fence was directly in line with fences 1 and 2, your horse would be running on a lot more.

Between fences 3 & 4, the rider should take advantage of the space to collect his thoughts and establish pace once again, concentrating on the course ahead. Apart from the geography of the ring as explained in approaching the last fence, the state of the going can also determine pace: the deeper the going, the shorter the

Fig 93   Van Der Valk, Working Hunter Pony of the Year 1974, ridden by Angela Massarella. Standing at 14.2hh, he pursued a successful show-jumping career after his Peterborough triumph.

stride and vice versa. Many course builders do not adjust the heights of the fences accordingly when the going is deep, although they should realize that fences in deep going artificially become three to six inches higher.

Beware of the temptation to give your horse too much room. He does not want reminding that the entrance is nearby, as you circle wide towards fence 4 (the bullfinch). All fences away from home (the entrance) need more determined riding to encourage the horse to go forward. Head for the middle of the bullfinch, motoring on at a good hunting pace so that there is no chance of your mount stopping at the last moment. If

fences such as these, ditches and water jumps are your problem fences, build one at home to practise over.

On landing after fence 4, unless you bear right, then left, on a straight approach into the parallel (5), you will automatically meet the fence on an angle, which is not advisable as the going is fairly deep and your horse may slither and fall. Always aim for the centre of the fence so that if your mount wavers in the approach, there is less chance of missing the fence out or hitting a wing.

The true parallel fence is more difficult to jump than the ascending one, especially this fence (5) as it seems to be all poles with no filling, showing plenty of daylight with no obvious groundline. If your horse can see objects from the ringside through the fence, it could necessitate giving him extra encouragement; a horse will automatically respect the more solid type of fence.

Soon after landing, there is quite a tight turn to the left, so go deep into the corner to allow maximum room for the double and do not sweep into an arc. In the short space of time given, try and collect him, without losing impulsion in the corner and get him back onto his hocks and listening to you, without losing forward momentum. Remember that the horse has cantered a big circle before meeting the bullfinch and then jumping the parallel, so he could be running on a bit, as well as being on his forehand and the double needs to be jumped with accuracy especially as the first element is a vertical with a mock ditch, which he will have down if he is sharp.

The distance between the two fences is greater than a bounce type combination which is better should your animal peep at the ditch (if the distance was a bounce which would mean your having to come in more slowly, your animal may stop altogether). My pony Cusop Emery became stuck in a dry ditch when hunter trialling and became genuinely frightened of them as a result. We built one at home to overcome this problem.

One of the most difficult fences is the next one (7), for which you have almost to double back on yourself (around the first fence) to jump well. It is an up-to-height fence of planks, and the downfall of careless jumpers. Slightly uphill and so soon after a 180-degree turn, you will really have to keep the momentum in order for the horse to meet the planks straight and accurately, with the horse

back on his hocks again, to make a good shape over the fence. Be accurate but not behind the movement, as a horse will automatically collect himself going uphill.

When landing there is no point in rushing; it is not as though you are jumping against the clock. Fence 8 is a staggered one of three jumps, off-line with a very short approach, at an angle from the ringside and with plenty of wispy greenery on the wings, which makes the combination look very spooky. The first part is open cross poles with no obvious groundline and plenty of daylight. Luckily, the animal is going towards home, but do not let him gallop on into this combination or you may become a hospital case at the third element. The trick with these types of fence is to find a straight line through them and, as with any fence with a short tight approach, keep the horse together with the engine running so that you do not run out of petrol on the turn into the first part; and be careful that the horse does not run out to the left straight towards the collecting ring – having a stick in the left hand as a warning may help.

Again, as you land, remember to keep concentrating even though there is a nice big sweep before fence 9; having got this far, you do not want to make a mess of the last few fences. How often do you see the jumping round spoilt at the last minute because the rider thought he was home and dry? To pass the entrance and jump fence 9 away from home, it will need determined riding, as it did when jumping fence 4, but this time even more so as your horse will be getting tired and may be looking back at the entrance as a result.

The next fence is certainly not a reward fence; it still requires a combination of capable horse and rider, and a cool head. However, it is one of the easiest of combinations: a parallel to a vertical to a parallel. The vertical in the middle gives your horse a slight breather, unlike the combination of two parallel fences placed together to make up either the first and second fences or the second and third fences, in a set of three. If you were faced with the latter combination, you would need plenty of impulsion to be sure of reaching the last two fences especially if they made up one of the last fences on the course. Many course builders usually make this one of the biggest, expecting the horses to jump well now that they are well warmed up.

The last fence, the stile, is perhaps the most difficult of all the course, not only because it has to be jumped with accuracy and follows a combination, but because the horse could be tired and agitated by the end of this series of tests. At least you can go deep into the corner around the first fence and bring the horse back off his hocks before approaching the fence on a nice steady, accurate stride, with the horse concentrating.

Stile fences are not usually very big, but are narrow instead, so must be jumped on a straight approach – definitely not on an angle otherwise you may take the wing with you.

Conclusion The course is definitely a testing, open one which you would wish to encounter later in the season, as there are some very tight turns and most of the fences make you think, although they do not discourage a flowing round. There are spreads and uprights mixed in with each other, which calls for more concentration (similar fences one after the other are far easier to jump and do not alter the pace too much).

The good points are that the ring is big enough and there are not too many fences, most of which are not up to height due to the heavy going. The first fences are heading towards home and the low wide parallel will encourage the horse to jump in a good shape. The solid fences have a variety of substantial filling, shrubbery, greenery and so on that complement the rustic fences and the distances between the combinations are true distances, encouraging a flowing round.

As soon as you have finished walking the course, return to your horse, which by now should have been got ready so that all there is to do is a final working in, prior to entering the ring. Sometimes the judges require all the class to enter prior to jumping, so that they have an idea as to the standard of class, so it pays to be ready even if you do not intend to jump until later on.

Whether you like to jump early or not (you may not have a choice as some classes run in catalogue order), it pays to watch a few rounds to give you an idea of how the course is riding; perhaps the staggered fence in our course is not riding as well as was thought or the stile is not proving to be a problem after all.

If your groundwork has been done well at home, your practice fences should be merely a warm-up to determine what sort of mood your animal is in on the day, or a chance to remind yourself about a particular type of fence that may exist in the course and that you may not have encountered for a while.

While in the collecting ring (apart from checking your girth once more), remind yourself also of the task in hand and go through the course in your mind once more. There is nothing worse than taking the wrong course which means elimination. I was in with a big chance at the Scottish Championships Show one year as my pony was jumping well despite the long journey. Just as I was giving myself a mental pat on the back after jumping what I thought was a competent clear round, a steward blew her whistle (so hard that I'm sure the pea nearly came out) to signal that I was eliminated because I had failed to jump the last fence, which was additional to the previous 14hh class which I had watched! – a case of learning a lesson the hard way.

When your time comes, either walk or trot smartly into the ring and give your number to the judge or steward saying either 'good morning' or 'afternoon', whichever is appropriate. Once given the go ahead to start (in some cases listen out for a whistle), use the next moments to establish a pace and attitude without circling the ring for what may seem like an eternity to the judge. First impressions are very important and are a good basis on which to start your round. The best advice is to remain calm and collected so that you can keep a clear head and recollect all your thoughts. Take each fence at a time with a view to the next fence in the forefront of your mind.

When you have completed your round, return to the judge as calmly as you approached – your style marks may not have been recorded at this point, so continue to keep your display nicely controlled and be pleasant and polite, no matter what has happened. Leave the ring calmly either at walk or trot. Do not gallop out of the ring as this will encourage your pony to bolt, possibly in the middle of a class another time. This advice also applies on a lap of honour.

Unless the judge asks for a gallop at the end of the round, do not bother, as this may only wind the horse up for the next phase and can often spoil a good impression. Instead, reward your pony, especially if he has performed well. Ideally, you want to leave the ring on a good note in preparation for the next time. Slipshod riding can lead to horses gradually developing bad habits associated with entering and leaving the ring. If things do go wrong, keep your composure which will help you rectify the problem. We have all been in this situation; do not see it as an affront to your personal ability and, in a blind panic, do something which you will regret or may land you in trouble with the governing society.

Style marks are very difficult to gain and often, are very easily lost (even if the horse jumps with a good shape) because the rider is untidy. As in normal showing, the rider should be as one with the horse and should not be noticed for the wrong reasons such as flapping and shouting.

Too often we see riders leaning either too far forwards (see Fig 94a) or too far backwards (see Fig 94b), often accompanied by hand, arm and leg positions

Fig 94(a) The rider leaning forwards.

Fig 94(b)   The rider leaning backwards.   *(c)   The rider sitting correctly.*

which are also incorrect, confusing the horse and putting him out of balance with it. Fig 94c shows a good position.

Riders that lean to one side or the other cause the horse to lose balance. This may be acceptable in motorbike racing but not in the show ring! However, perhaps one of the worst sights are those jockeys who have their reins too fixed and, when losing balance over a fence, give their poor horses what is known as 'a dentist job'. Also, if reins, which are the communication lines, are too long and held in a tight hand, the slack rein catches the horse in the mouth.

Any problems need to be eliminated before they become habit forming. Problems with riders are in many ways easier to sort out than equine ones although both can usually be overcome by a process of elimination. If a horse appears to have a problem, it may be that the ground is too hard, or that he has a splint coming, or sore shins; or he may need his teeth or back checking; or it is simply the fact that the rider has allowed the horse to get

away with murder more and more each time in the ring. This is one reason that you must always, when leaving the ring, think about repairing any damage done for the next time. Sometimes problems arise because the horse is physically incapable of performing the task that has been asked of him – a good case for not overfacing your horse at any level and making sure that your horse is fit enough to cope with the demands of his work schedule.

The running out problem (like the rushing one) is a difficult one to cure with an inexperienced rider and is often a result of the rider being 'overhorsed'. The first thing is to control the speed to prevent the horse running and secondly, to put a more competent jockey on board. Then work out to which side the horse favours when running out. If, for instance, he favours the left, put the stick in the left hand and if he attempts to do it, use the whip sharply on the left side immediately (not five minutes later) and turn him to the right. With the rushing problem,

117

either into a fence or on landing, common sense applies here and the rider must regulate the pace, even turning the horse away from the fence on approach to make him think, or halting immediately after landing.

If a pony refuses, often the two most common causes are that firstly, a pony has lost his confidence for whatever reason (a youngster may have been over-faced). Dealing with this problem usually entails starting a rehabilitation course and returning to basics whether it be small fence work gradually building up to the particular larger fence that is causing the problem in the hope of regaining his confidence, or returning to a loose jumping lane, or simply giving the horse a rest (particularly if he has been over-shown). The second common cause is the fault of the rider who puts the horse into fences wrongly, either at a bad angle or at too slow or fast a speed, or by dropping rein contact immediately in front of a jump causing the young or unbalanced horse to scramble on to his forehand at the crucial moment.

A good piece of advice I shall always remember is that the good rider always waits for the fence to come to him and should keep motoring, preferably in gear. In other words, the horse is not running on at fast speed but the rider is controlling the power and impulsion at the right speed to enable the horse to jump the obstacle accurately.

Even though it can be argued that on a true working hunter or working hunter pony course, the rider should be going at a hunting pace and not as a showjumper, it is important that a rider should be able to see a stride to some extent and also be aware of his horse's length of stride, especially for the bigger fences and com-

binations. I was always told that, if seeing a stride was a major problem, riding a grade A schoolmaster would go a long way to teaching you to see one and to give the correct aid at the right moment for take-off.

Other problems such as clumsiness, having poles down (known as the four-faulter) and jumping in a wrong shape, often reveal themselves at a later date because shortcuts have been taken in the initial stages of training, which all necessitates a return to basic schooling. Most horses and ponies have some natural ability and can jump up to a certain level quite capably. However, this ability will often disappear when the fences become considerably more demanding and then, in some cases, you realize that your animal is not a top competition horse after all. Although some horses, even at a higher level, have more natural ability than others, most animals have to be taught, and success has resulted from a sound early training programme executed over a gradual length of time.

Training the Working Pony

The training of the horse is very similar to teaching jockeys and good results are achieved with a step-by-step approach.

Before attempting any jumping training, your horse must be well schooled on the flat, which is the basis for ultimate control when jumping. If your horse is obedient to your hand and leg and working correctly, this will not only help you to place him more accurately into the fences, as well as improve your technique over them, but also determine what happens between the fences, often the part in the round when careless riders lose valuable style marks. The horse needs to be in total balance, going forward, with plenty of impulsion, so that the stride can be shortened and lengthened and the horse turned at a moment's notice.

When starting his education over fences, it is far better for your animal if you gradually teach correct technique over smaller fences rather than overface him with big fences and demanding distances too early on in an impatient effort to test his ability under pressure or to see what he is really made of. Little by little, the fences can be made more testing, but only if the horse has fully understood the previous work and jumped with confidence and enjoyment.

As in any area of training, the good trainer knows when to proceed to the next stage, being neither too cautious and running the risk of boring the horse, nor rushing the training so that the horse frightens himself by struggling to jump a fence when he is not ready for it. The golden rules are: reward him when he has done well; and quickly make amends to regain his confidence when problems occur by either sympathetic or firm handling. Remember, an animal's jumping progress is very easy to spoil.

It makes sense to introduce your horse to poles on the ground during your flat work. They will make him supple, develop his sense of rhythm, keep him alert and athletic, and help him to become accustomed to poles in preparation for jumping training. In early stages, poles will guide him into fences and, later on, regulate his stride, particularly before take-off and in combinations and related distance exercises.

When starting over poles and cavalletti, begin with one and gradually introduce three or four more, so that when a simple cross pole fence is constructed at the end of the pole lane, it will seem like a natural progression to the horse. Have an assistant close at hand to adjust the distances between the poles when they become dislodged or need altering to suit the individual requirements of the horse at different paces or when teaching your animal to lengthen or shorten strides. There are no hard and fast rules but if the distance appears wrong, change it at once. (Basic distances can be found in any good jumping book.) Gradually increase the size of this last fence, both in height and spread, so that you can then move on to single fences, which should be solid and inviting to promote confidence and ability.

At the same time as tackling single fences, whether they be uprights or spreads, return to a more sophisticated type of grid work as training progresses to teach the animal to jump doubles and combinations on different strides and at different heights. Some people like to continue grid work after basic pole and cavalletti work and tackle single fences later on. Either way, the correctly constructed grid will teach the horse to think as well as provide wonderful gymnastic exercises, which will make him more athletic. Schooling a young horse over a grid has been compared to teaching a child to construct a sentence from single words.

When the horse works confidently through the many varieties of grids and can jump a variety of single fences in a good outline, neither rushing nor spooking, the next stage is to introduce him to a small course of fences, which is what all the work has been leading up to. This may seem an easy task in theory but, in practice, the horse has to realize that the single fences are now approaching one after the other (not in a straight line as in a grid) and possibly with tight approaches and angles and so on.

When first starting to jump, many trainers (apart from those who always prefer to school from on top) believe that horses are better off without riders, especially if the riders have little experience over fences. They believe that it teaches the horse to think for himself, without the encumbrance of the extra weight, promoting self-confidence in his own ability.

Some experts prefer jumping on the lunge, saying that they have more control in regulating pace and approaches and believing that the horse is more relaxed since he is already accustomed to being schooled on the lunge from the breaking days. Other trainers think that loose jumping is safer (no chance of the lunge line tangling in the fences) and teaches animals to jump more freely than on a lungeing circle.

Most people opt for lungeing as they often do not have the schooling facilities for loose jumping. An important point to remember, however, is that the handler must be very active and move quickly so that the horse can have the freedom to lower his head when jumping, as well as allowing the horse to meet the fence in the right place. Make sure that the wings are low so that the lunge line can move freely over the fence and that they invite the horse into the fence, discouraging running out.

When jumping loose in an enclosed area like an indoor school, make sure the horse cannot jump out of the lane and that there are enough assistants to keep the horse moving, especially on the corners, without frightening him, which will en-courage him to become excitable and teach him to rush his fences. As with all schooling, it is better to achieve good results in a short space of time than to overwork a tired horse. Once the horse is jumping loose in a relaxed manner, the competent rider can take over the controls. He will be invaluable (especially to the horse who lacks self-confidence), in helping to keep the rhythm, maintain impulsion and reassure the horse in the approach to the fence, especially when the time comes to meet more difficult and daunting ones.

If the training programme is going according to plan, there will come a time when the working pony/working hunter will need to see a little more of life, either by attending a show or a hunt, or a hunter trial. All these help to broaden a horse's education and it will give you more of an indication of your horse's ability. (It is also a good way to sweeten up an older, experienced horse.) Hunting (and cross-country competitions) will teach your horse to jump bolder, in an on-going pace, meeting more natural obstacles such as water ditches, drop fences, bullfinch type hedges and dark woods, than you could set up at home. Most competent course builders make good use of uneven ground at shows and so the unexpected drops and sloping approaches you meet out hunting will give you valuable practice.

No matter how exciting the run, you must not allow your horse to jump flat and gallop off (especially with the novice) and remember that, in this instance, you are using the hunting field for schooling. If your young horse becomes unsettled out hunting on the first couple of outings, you can either hunt him hard until he becomes accustomed to it or, perhaps

Fig 95   Rajah III, the very first Working Hunter of the Year in retirement with Ronnie Marmont in the Quorn Monday country.

more wisely, keep him home. Ill-mannered horses are unwelcome both in the hunting field and in the show ring; some who are quiet in the show ring can be quite dangerous in the hunting field and vice versa – although the common cause is often that the horse has not been introduced to hounds correctly. It is common sense to go to a quiet meet at the beginning.

Although your prospective working hunter may come on in leaps and bounds while hunting, it may be necessary to do some show jumping (although not against the clock), as an alternative discipline. The former will encourage him to jump in a free style, which is what you should do in the show ring and the latter will teach the young horse to be more accurate and, most importantly, teach him to jump in cold blood. It is surprising how many grand performers

121

*Fig 96 Something Original (15hh), Working Hunter Pony of
the Year 1988 ridden by fifteen-year-old Adele Atkinson, who
also won the title the following year with her 14hh mare
Autumn Rose.*

in the hunting field find the show ring
a poor substitute and do not excel as a
result.

When the time comes to compete in the
show ring, do not expect to win at the
very beginning. Use your first season to
introduce your animal properly to the
various situations, thinking of the future.
You will get more credit in the long run
for bringing a new animal on slowly,
than overjumping a horse who is left
burnt out before he even gets his life
height certificate.

The BSPS competitors are indeed fortunate to be able to enjoy a winter season
in which they can bring on their novice
animals gradually. Their horse colleagues have only the hunting field and
the showjumping ring in which to
monitor their horses' training and progress. Jumping is a specialist subject and
my advice is that if at any time you feel
that you are not capable of sorting out
problems or going any further with a
training programme, seek help from the
experts.

Working Hunter Pony of the Year at The BSPS Championship Show from 1968

1968	Beckfield Ben Hur	1979	Toyd Bewildered
1969	Beckfield Ben Hur	1980	Twyford Cracker
1970	Tonto	1981	Sefton Tony of Alderbourne
1971	Tonto	1982	Nutbeam Minto
1972	Beckfield Ben Hur	1983	Nutbeam Minto
1973	Leamington Carello	1984	Just Jasper
1974	Van der Valk	1985	Little Diamond
1975	Caerloew Planet	1986	Sandman
1976	Coalport	1987	Towy Valley Maurice
1977	Rookery Jigsaw	1988	Something Original
1978	Lynscott Medallion	1989	Autumn Rose

Working Hunter of the Year at The Horse of the Year Show from 1951

1951	Rajah III	1971	Someday
1952	Lanhill	1972	Sporting Print
1953	Rajah III	1973	Slaney Valley
1954	Pampas Cat	1974	Mister Perkins
1955		1975	Fidelio
1956	No classes held	1976	Morning Glory
1957		1977	Let's Go
1958	Robin Wood II	1978	Let's Go
1959	Ryebrooks	1979	Castlewellan
1960	Fintan	1980	Dual Gold
1961	Navan	1981	Andeguy
1962	Makeway	1982	Cartier
1963	Rhythm	1983	Gibbethill
1964	Sundew	1984	Threes are Wild
1965	Kittiwake	1985	Supercoin
1966	Rupert	1986	Valindrie
1967	Snake	1987	Lifeline
1968	Sebastian	1988	Boleyhill
1969	Goodwill	1989	Bootleg
1970	Upton		

6 Outside the Ring

Running a showing yard is a very time-consuming job and requires someone with a talent for organization. Apart from arranging everyday activities such as feeding, exercising, and staff rotas etc., flu vaccinations, blacksmith visits, height measurements, registrations and memberships have also to be renewed and keeping up to date with show entries is a demanding business so a large desk diary is a must in a busy showing stable – much easier than relying on memory.

If a show animal is worked correctly, fed accordingly, and groomed and strapped well, his shape and appearance should automatically look presentable over a period of time. If an animal is not well inside, he will seldom look well on the outside, as condition and bloom come from within. Good feeding is an art perfected with experience although, nowadays, it is becoming more scientific in top-class performance circles, particularly in the USA, Australia and on the Continent. Each individual horseman has his own special way of feeding, his biggest problem being when a horse in the peak of condition stops eating, (which is usually when this happens).

Feeding

Feeding is a question of balance. Food quantity should relate to body-weight and the intended activity, but the feeder should also be aware of the strength of the different foodstuffs, which is not always easy to determine in coarse mix feeds. Horses like something to pick at (otherwise psychologically caused vices will develop) and then they grind down the food many times. Because they are chewing animals, it is important that teeth are regularly checked.

Apart from having small stomachs, horses have a low enzyme count which does not allow concentrates to break down as readily – the advantage of processed food is that it is especially formulated to allow for this – so feed little and often. Hansom cab owners used to feed a handful of food to their horses fourteen times a day.

Grass contains a high percentage of water, which is one reason that stabled horses should have plenty of water available. Although, up to a point, most horse owners can judge hay for themselves, it may be a wise move to have hay analysed if it is part of a scientific concentrated diet. Required roughage ratios vary from 100 per cent roughage for the ordinary pony, to 20 per cent roughage 80 per cent concentrates for the top performance horse. Earlier cut hay is more valuable nutritionally as there is more leaf than stem (60 per cent of the feed value is in the leaves). New hay can be fed once it has become stabilized. Some people soak hay if their horse suffers from respiratory problems. However, there is no need to oversoak it otherwise all the goodness is left in the soup; just lightly soak it to keep the spores and dust down so that they do not affect the respiratory tracts.

One of the major considerations in any showing yard is to be aware of horses coming into contact with any forbidden substances which may show up in a positive dope test, such as vitamins, veterinary products and leg washes and so on.

Presuming your horse looks a picture of health and is going beautifully in his work, the next stage is to concentrate on the finer points of production such as the horse's turn-out for the ring. It is the attention to detail that usually achieves success.

Grooming

Trimming the show animal (preferably with the small clippers) gives a neater outline and creates a complimentary picture, although you should check that trimming is permitted by your show society. However, done badly, this can be disastrous. Too long a tail will give the appearance of a long pony, trimming along the backs of the legs could make your horse look light of bone and being too adventurous with the scissors on the mane at the poll and wither can take away valuable plaiting space which is a bad thing if your animal is short of front in the first place. Too much scissoring at the poll can make the head look plain. Conversely, clever plaiting can improve the neck line greatly, high plaits which sit on top of the neck will appear to give the horse more crest and tight plaits which sit below the crest line, the opposite. If the portion of mane used is of even length and thickness, the plaits should be identical in shape and size and the more plaits there are, the longer the front will appear to the eye.

High Plaits   (see Fig 97)

Start by dividing each portion of mane into three equal parts with the comb (see Fig 97a) and begin to plait about 1½ inches from the roots, locking the hair quite tightly in an upward motion (see Fig 97b). Secure the end of the plait with needle and thread (Fig 97c) and also gather any loose ends otherwise these will reappear like a paintbrush (Fig 97d). Sew the needle under and through the plait about 2 inches from the roots (Fig 97e), wrap the cotton around the plait away from the roots and put the needle through the end (Fig 97f). The sewn plait is now half the length but double the thickness at this stage. Roll and mould the plait into a ball and secure firmly by sewing into place, being careful not to damage the hood effect you have created at the roots (Fig 97g).

Tight Plaits   (see Fig 98)

Begin as before, but plait from the roots, pulling downwards, pressing with the thumbs to maintain tension (to stop the plait from coming loose when rolling up) (Fig 98a). Secure as normal and thread the needle as close to the neck as possible (Figs 98b and c). Then include any loose hair either side of the plait to eliminate the hood effect (Fig 98d), before wrapping the cotton around the double thickness plait as before (Fig 98e). Roll the plait into a ball and secure this so that it rests on the side of the neck below the top line. Loop the cotton either side of the plait for extra security, flattening any hood effect which may appear (Fig 98f).

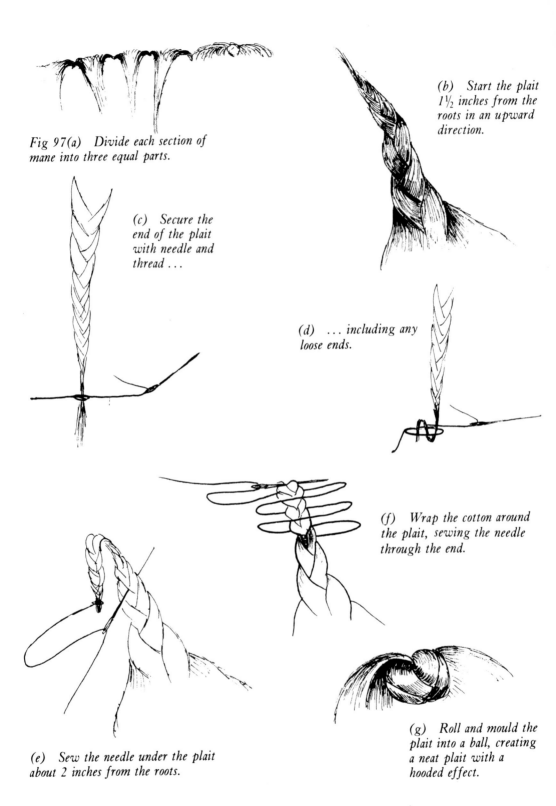

Fig 97(a)   Divide each section of mane into three equal parts.

(b)   Start the plait 1½ inches from the roots in an upward direction.

(c)   Secure the end of the plait with needle and thread ...

(d)   ... including any loose ends.

(f)   Wrap the cotton around the plait, sewing the needle through the end.

(e)   Sew the needle under the plait about 2 inches from the roots.

(g)   Roll and mould the plait into a ball, creating a neat plait with a hooded effect.

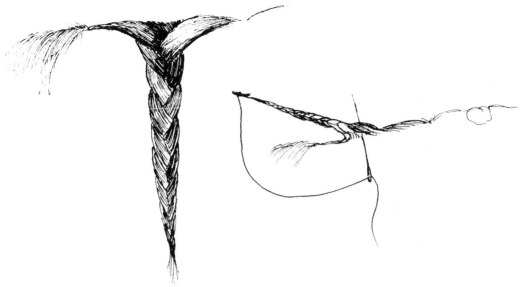

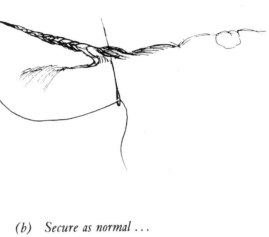

98(a)   Plait tightly from the roots in a downward direction.

(b)   Secure as normal ...

(c)   ... threading the needle close to the neck.

(d)   Include loose hair at the top of the plait.

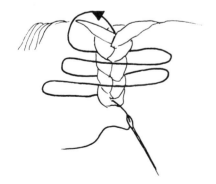

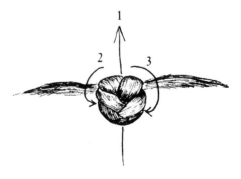

(e)   Wrap the cotton around the plait, sewing the needle through the bottom.

(f)   Secure the rolled plait and stitch down any hood effect either side.

127

Fig 99   An ordinary tail plait.

Tail Plaiting

I personally prefer to see a well-pulled tail. However, plaited tails, done well, look the part in some of the in hand classes.

To achieve a really neat tail plait requires patience, practice and a good grip. The tail hairs must be of sufficient length at the sides so that they will stay in place securely once plaited, and must be clean and very well combed out all the way down.

A tail that has been rubbed at the top is difficult to plait neatly, as you have to start a little further down to find hairs long enough to get the plait started, resulting in a tufty appearance at the top. Over-tight plaiting can result in the skin becoming very sore and scabby, and the animal may become distressed the next time the tail is combed out or plaited again and will be uncomfortable in the ring.

The technique for a raised plait is slightly different from that used for plaiting a tail normally (where the sections from alternate sides are crossed over each other like mane plaiting as you work down the tail (*see* Fig 99)). For a raised plait, the sections must be taken from under and behind each other. The difference is easy to see when watching someone carry out this method.

1.   Take a small and even section of hair from each side (*see* Fig. 100a) and cross them left over right (*see* Fig 100b).
2.   With the right thumb holding these sections firmly crossed on the right forefinger, the left hand introduces a third section from the left side which is also held temporarily in the right hand but not bunched with sections 1 and 2 (*see* Fig 100c).
3.   The left hand takes hold of section 2 from the right side and brings it down over to the left; at the same time the left thumb pushes section 3 up into the centre and holds all sections (*see* Fig 100d).
4.   The right hand brings in section 4 from the right side to join with section 1 (*see* Fig 100d).
5.   The forefinger of the right hand brings section 3 down and across (*see* Fig 100e). At the same time, the thumb of the right hand pushes sections 4 and 1 (now bunched together) up into the centre (*see* Fig 100f).
6.   Continue taking sections in this manner (Fig 100g), working with your hands as close to the tail as possible so that the side pieces do not become longer and loose as you progress down the tail. If

(b) Cross left over right.

Fig 100(a) Take an equal small section of hair from each side.

(e) Now put 3 over 1 and 4.

(c) Introduce a third section from the left side.

(d) Bring 2 over 3 and take another small section, 4, from the right to join 1.

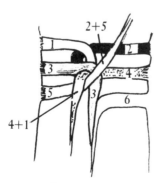

(f) Lift 1 and 4 up between 2 and 3 and introduce 5 from the left to join 2.

(g) Drop 1 and 4 over 5 and 2 and introduce 6 from the right to join 3.

(h) At the end of the dock, or when plait is the required length, plait all loose ends together.

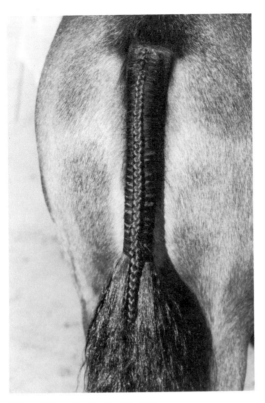

Fig 101   A raised tail plait.

large sections are taken in from the side, the centre plait will become bulky and difficult to manage.

7.   Once the end of the dock has been reached, stop taking in the side sections and continue making one long plait in the same way, wrapping each piece round behind the other (*see* Fig 100h). Secure the end neatly with needle and thread by wrapping the thread round over folded-over spiky ends. The bound end is then taken up and tucked tidily under the last half an inch of the main tail plait and the needle and thread is taken through both thicknesses of plait using small stitches to secure. The loop of free plait is then stitched down its length so that it will lie flat and tidy, not as a loose loop and the thread is sewn in at the end with a knot.

8.   Spray lightly with hairspray (or apply setting gel). Bandage to flatten down any stray hairs and to protect the plait. Only bandage as far down as the last side sections and use a stocking to protect the rest of the tail so that you are not left with a bandage indentation ring around the tail hairs lower down. Also remember to unravel the bandage when removing and do not pull off as with a pulled tail.

Tail plaiting is useful to improve the appearance of foals' tails for showing; and for youngsters that are only going to be shown a few times, it saves having to pull the tail. If the same tail is plaited repeatedly to do a lot of shows, the hairs can break off, making it more difficult to plait neatly the next time.

Quarter Marks

Quarter marks (*see* Fig 104) are not merely for decoration. Used correctly (which comes with practice) they can improve quarters which are very flat, slope away, or lack condition or scope. They are achieved by combing or brushing the coat in different directions, using a fairly stiff body brush and a varied selection of combs as a bigger horse will require larger squares than a lead-rein pony. Block type squares are more suitable for the more workman-like classes (*see* Fig 102a).

To give the patterns more definition, use a wet sponge to dampen the hair beforehand (*see* Fig 102b) or even setting gel. The golden rule is to start the line of squares so that they are parallel to the ground line and not the shape of the quarters (*see* Fig 102c) and to reproduce the same effect on both sides (*see* Fig 102d).

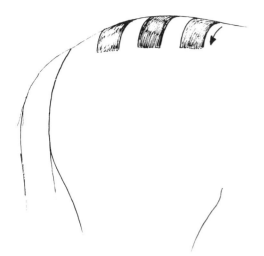

Fig 102(a)   Block-type squares.

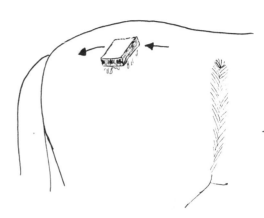

(b)   Dampen hair beforehand to give patterns more definition.

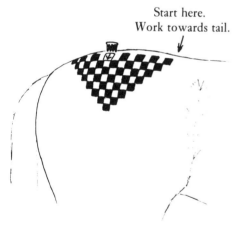

(c)   Starting line of squares should be parallel to the ground line.

(d)   Produce a symmetrical pattern on both sides.

Sharks teeth can be used to fill a hollow flank and make a weak second thigh look stronger (*see* Fig 103a), and brush marks (*see* Fig 103b) make the quarters look stronger and symmetrical when standing behind although they need to be drawn cleverly otherwise they can break up a quarter badly.

The Finishing Touches

There is no point in chalking white socks, hoof-oiling feet, spraying show gloss on the coat or putting brilliantine on the tail if your animal is not clean in the first place. Clear setting gel is ideal for keeping plaits and patterns in place and most

131

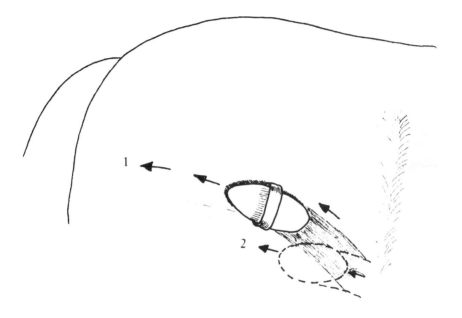

Fig 103(a)   Using a stiff bodybrush, brush coat in different directions ...

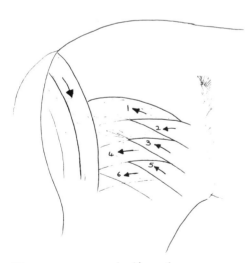

(b)   ... to create a shark's tooth effect and a brush line.

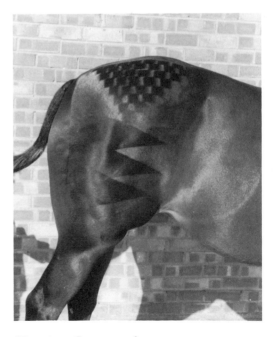

Fig 104   Quartermarks.

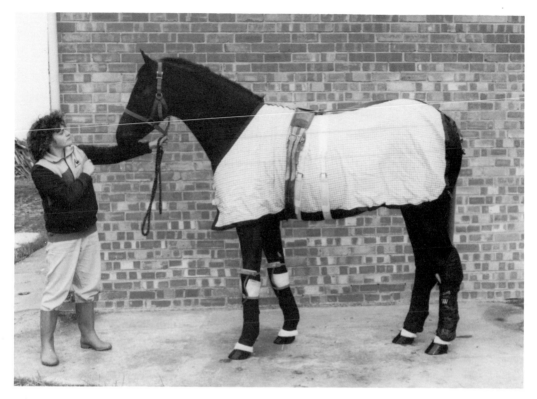

Fig 105 A horse prepared for travelling on a warm day . . .

successful on tails prior to bandaging. We use black stage make up in crayon form to discreetly highlight the eyes and muzzle, blended in with liquid paraffin or baby oil rather than sticky petroleum jelly which attracts the dust. We have also had great success with fly repellant in spray form (which is essential on some show days) to avoid a blotchy finish.

Travelling

Show stock should be well bandaged and appropriately rugged (*see* Figs 105–6) when travelling to shows. Partitions rather than bars should be used and adjusted according to your horse's individual requirements. Also, the horse-box should be well bedded down with straw to lessen the risk of injury, especially when transporting foals. Looking after stock while in transit is extremely important; checking that they are not too hot or cold during the extremes of the long show day, supplying them with hay, a drink of water and the occasional feed as well as careful driving will ensure that not too much is taken out of the animals travelling either to or from the show. After all, there is no point in having a show horse that will not travel well.

Clothes

Showing is all about presentation, and so it makes sense that you should be cor-

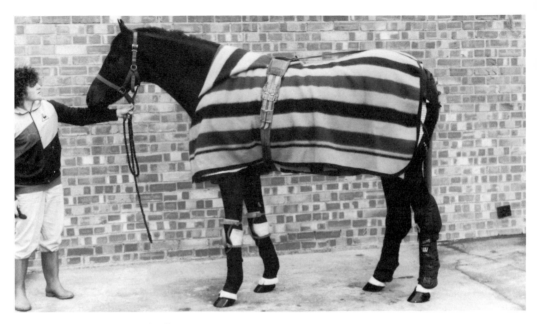

Fig 106 ... and on a cold day.

rectly and smartly turned out, otherwise there is little point in having your horse looking fabulous. Apart from the fact that looking untidy will do little for your confidence in the ring (something the showman must never lack), it reflects badly on your own standard of management at home and your attitude towards the judge. In fact, I would go as far as to say that an average rider or one of awkward shape can look more accomplished by being turned out elegantly.

One of the advantages of this hobby is that you can watch the experts in the ring nearly every week, so that if you are in doubt as to what is deemed correct, watch the respective classes for guidance.

Adult Classes

In hunter, hack and cob classes, men should wear the traditional ratcatcher, which consists of long boots, breeches, bowler hat, shirt and tie and a tweed jacket (the latter with not too loud a check otherwise it will draw attention away from the horse). There is nothing to stop lady riders wearing the same including a bowler hat, although many wear a navy jacket (black can look sombre) often with a navy velvet collar matching the shade of their riding cap. An alternative idea, which can look very smart for the ladies, is a tweed jacket with a velvet collar and matching velvet cap. Although the show ring is deemed a conservative place as far as fashion is concerned, any new idea is welcomed as long as it is in keeping with Robert Oliver's saying, 'the best-dressed person is the one who draws the least attention'. Some ladies often add a touch of their own individuality, not wishing to look like an exact copy of the twenty or so other riders in the ring.

At this point, I would advise ladies in hack classes with noticeable tummies to avoid the cut-away jackets which are worn more in final performances. A well-cut jacket can do much to make the rider look stylish and the Bernard Weatherall ones are probably the best, although they can also be expensive especially when the travelling for fittings is also taken into account. A cheaper alternative is to use a local tailor although he must be made aware that, compared to ordinary sports jackets, riding ones are usually slightly skirted and longer (especially in the sleeves so that not too much shirt cuff is revealed when the arms are bent) and that they must retain their shape when riding. If you are a standard shape and height, off-the-peg jackets can be an even cheaper alternative and are improving in quality all the time; a few years ago, I would have suggested finding a second-hand garment instead, as brand new jackets could not match them for quality. I have never been a fan of the washable jackets either, nor the variety of coloured ones.

Although hats come in all shapes and sizes and it is important that you choose one that suits your face and stature (i.e. not too tall a riding cap or wide a bowler), above all, wear one that fits well. I remember an incident at a Scottish show years ago when a steward would not let my brother into the jumping ring with his working hunter pony Downland Smuggler because he did not have elastic under his chin. I pointed out to him that it was a Herbert Johnson riding cap which had been made to measure and so did not require an elastic chinstrap. Nowadays, in working hunter pony classes, skull caps must be worn in the jumping phase, but the wearing of a back protector is one of personal choice.

Off-white, buff or very pale lemon jodhpurs or breeches are more suitable for the show ring than white or canary yellow and, since the advent of the washable stretch variety, there should be no difficulty in finding a pair that is comfortable to wear. To be correct, there should be two small buttons just below and on the outside of the knee to accommodate the garter strap of the long boots which should have the buckle fastened between the buttons.

Probably the most difficult item of riding wear to find nowadays is a good pair of long boots that will last a lifetime. A good quality made-to-measure pair can represent an expensive outlay and many of the new ready-made pairs (which take a long time to break in before they become less like a plaster cast) are usually poor quality and do not fit well. If you do not mind the thought of stepping into someone else's shoes, so to speak, your best bet for value for money may be to scout around for a second-hand pair, complete with trees. A pair of boots that are deemed a good fit are those which are a snug fit neither too tight, which causes undue pain, nor so slack that you can put your hand down the side.

To be correct, spurs should be worn with long boots (not in BSPS classes) even if these are the dummy variety although I would suggest this depends on your horse, remembering that judges do not wear them. One often sees these worn incorrectly either at half mast, or even upside down, and do remember to have the buckles of the spur strap at the front on the outside of the instep.

All items of riding wear will last longer and look their best if well cared for, which entails putting jackets on hangers with bulky items removed from pockets and replacing trees in clean boots after use.

135

One of the worst sights in the show ring, in both adults' and children's classes, involves the humble shirt and tie and, luckily, there are now more firms, obviously aware of the demand, selling a varied selection of decent showing shirts around the shows. Too often, shirt collars resemble stale bread or are too big around the neck and are accompanied by extra long sleeves and ties that resemble unruly scarves. There is nothing smarter than a well-fitting shirt with a crisp clean collar complemented by a silk tie (in a neat windsor knot) which should not be seen flapping about in faster paces. In children's classes, the colour combination of the pony's browband is often matched with girls' hair ribbons, which, incidentally, should be neat and not resemble Christmas wrapping.

In the WHP and SHP classes, there are more tweed coats being worn than navy blue ones and some of the male riders also sport bowler hats which look smart and in keeping with the nature of the classes. Many riders complete the picture by wearing waistcoats which can be rather bulky and uncomfortable when riding in hot weather.

Some children in the latter classes have swapped the normal leather-covered showing cane for a junior size hunting whip, sometimes bound with cotton for easier carrying. All canes and sticks should conform to the regulation length and it goes without saying that a smaller cane will suit a younger child while the hunter professional will require a more robust accessory. A lot of hack riders carry extra long canes which they rest on their inside knee when riding one-handed.

In the children's classes, most of the riders wear either black or brown jodphur boots and a good tip is to put a strip of elastic of matching colour sewn to the hem of the jodphurs under the boot to keep the jodphurs in place and lessen the risk of revealing the socks. It is quite permissible for the teenage riders to wear long boots and if these have to be the good-quality rubber ones, polishing them with proper shoe polish rather than with furniture polish will create a matt finish and make them look more like real leather ones.

Leather or hogskin gloves are ideal for showing and the unlined ones give a better feeling of contact with your horse. In wet weather when the reins are slippery, you may be better with a pair of string or wool gloves (those with rubber grips on the palms are the best), or you could dispense with gloves altogether.

To complete the picture, a fresh buttonhole rather than a plastic one looks the part, sometimes matching the colour combinations. For instance, our jockeys wear a neat red buttonhole carnation securely pinned from underneath the lapel and definitely without a long stalk, fern or silver paper. Strictly speaking, these should not be worn in any of the hunter type classes. Although *de rigeur* in today's showing classes, flowers were originally worn by ladies riding in the park as a sign that they had accepted the wooing of their admirers who used to send flowers to the houses of young ladies, which was considered socially acceptable. While mothers would decide which flowers would be worn or carried at the balls every evening, often sent by the most eligible suitor, the young ladies themselves would choose the buttonholes worn on the morning ride in the park. Violets were always worn by young ladies at the opening meet.

In the WHP and SHP Championships

at the RIHS, and in the evening at the BSPS Winter Championship Show, children are expected to dress more formally, which means a navy blue or black jacket accompanied by a hunting tie more commonly but wrongly called a stock which should also be secured with two pins at both ends to keep it in place in addition to the visible stock pin.

Many of the children rise to these important occasions and look splendid. In the adult final performance classes, ladies have an easier time than the gentlemen riders and require the same as the children i.e. a dark jacket, hunting tie (with not too fancy a stock pin) together with a top hat.

In hunter and cob classes final performances, gentlemen are expected to wear full hunting dress, which consists of either a longer hunting coat or the Johnny Walker style coat, with a waistcoat, top hat, hunting tie and hunting whip. If a scarlet coat is to be worn, white breeches and mahogany-top boots with white garter straps are in order.

In hack classes, park dress is compulsory. This consists of a black morning coat, grey striped or black close-fitting military trousers or overalls, with a shirt and tie or cravat, waistcoat and black jodphur boots or jemimas which have a spur fitted to them. A pair of hogskin gloves, a showing cane and a small buttonhole will complete the picture.

In riding horse classes, some riders opt for park dress, while others wear the Johnny Walker outfit (sometimes with a buttonhole and always with a normal showing cane).

Mrs Ben Harwood says the only way to clean a silk top hat is to use steam and silk. Her method, which has been handed down from generation to generation since Victorian times, is to hold the hat well away from a steaming kettle and then smooth over the hat (going with the pile not against it) with a piece of silk cloth. The hat is guaranteed to 'come up' beautifully.

Some of the most comical sights to be seen in the ring belong to the handlers in the leading rein classes. The art is to look smart without under or over selling yourself so that you neither make the picture look miserable nor look like something from a Royal Garden Party. The picture should be tasteful and harmonious; often the colour scheme of the pony's browband and rider's outfit is carried through to the handler. Unruly hats (also seen being worn by some of the less experienced lady judges), unsuitable footwear and badly fitting suits (on both males and females) can ruin the overall impression and performance.

There are no set rules in the in hand classes and, consequently, we see an enormous variety of outfits (especially in the hat department) reflecting varying degrees of effort made by the exhibitors. For example, men's clothes range from suits with bowlers to vests and trainers! Although I can appreciate that it is difficult to remain spick and span when closely involved with unpredictable youngsters, it is worth noting that when certain classes award points for presentation, some handlers are almost unrecognizable in their new attire and it is sad that this high standard of turn-out cannot be maintained all the time. Never having been a great admirer of swishy dressage whips on showgrounds, I particularly do not like to see them being used on youngsters in the ring – much better to carry a leather covered cane.

Similarly, I do think that there should

be some guide-lines laid down by shows regarding the dress of grooms in the ring since these outfits vary enormously. If more stewards took the same stand as Dennis Colton does at the London shows, the show ring would be a far better place. If judges, stewards, sponsors and most exhibitors make a concerted effort to turn themselves out well, thus maintaining a high standard – all for the good of showing – then why should those few who cannot be bothered be allowed to let the side down including, in some instances, their own animals.

Saddlery

Just as turning yourself out incorrectly can reflect badly on the overall production, so too can showing in dirty, ill-fitting tack. It is also worth remembering that clever use of tack can improve the way of going of the animal and, consequently, the ride and the feel a jockey (as well as the judge) obtains. At a Judge's Conference recently, one eminent hack judge said that the tack on a horse can often give the very important first impression when he gets on board. Certain items of tack can also alter the true picture just as unsuitable tack can reveal many weaknesses in conformation.

The most difficult item of saddlery equipment to find is a suitable saddle and those that fit a large number of horses and ponies are worth their weight in gold. The ideal saddle for showing is a straight cut one so that the shoulder is exposed more, giving the impression that the horse has more length of rein. However, many of the soup-plate flat types are slippery and uncomfortable to ride in, giving the judge a bad impression or a

younger jockey a feeling of insecurity. The best saddles range from the old traditional Owen saddles, which fit almost anything, to those with a slight knee roll. There are also more dressage saddles being worn, but these must not be perched too high on the horse's back as most riders, especially hunter judges, like to feel they are close to the horse.

When choosing a saddle for your horse, remember that they come in all shapes and weights and sizes and that saddle flaps can also make all the difference to the appearance. A big wide flap could easily drown your horse, giving the appearance of lacking scope and depth whereas too small a flap could make the horse look gutty. Similarly, a big saddle can disguise a long back and we often use a slightly smaller saddle on the ponies that are very short-coupled to give them more definition. However this is not possible in horse classes as the judge must also be accommodated – a very important point as he may refuse to ride an exhibit if he considers the saddle to be unsuitable, either because it is too small in the seat or because the stirrups are too small and leathers not long enough. I have actually seen this happen when a hunter judge would not ride a horse in a dressage saddle that was not suited to his traditional style of riding (a forward leg position).

I can never understand why some exhibitors show horses side-saddle in normal astride classes because even though the horses may go better this way, the judges are still having to ride them astride, apart from the fact that the swap over is a nuisance. More general-purpose type saddles that do not cover the shoulder too much are ideal for the working classes and give the rider more security over the bigger fences. I can never understand why parents expect small children who are not particularly secure in the seat, to jump in showing saddles.

At one time, white girths appeared to be the norm (except for hunter type classes), particularly those nasty, narrow webbing ones that appeared to cut the pony in two. Nowadays, exhibitors are using darker coloured girths, probably being aware that a white girth, although at times can look very striking especially in hack classes, can also visually break up the outline which is not a good thing if your animal has, say, a better front than quarters – much better in this case for the tack to blend in.

At Blue Slate, we are using the cottage craft girths more and more and have always favoured leather three-fold and balding girths on the big horses. We never use the standard dressage girths, which look like Houdini's stage props, but have the dressage saddle's girth-straps shortened so that a standard girth can be used instead. On all of the saddles that have three girth-straps, we use the first and third ones and feel this keeps the saddle in place. After all, who wants to ride in a saddle that shifts around? All too often they can be seen slipping forwards. If a girth has a middle plate, make sure that this remains in the middle by tightening up the girth on both sides.

Another present-day fashion (and I use the word deliberately as I firmly believe many people copy the experts even if it is not necessary) is the over-use of numnahs which must be secured under the saddle and not be tight over the wither region. Ideal for horses that are cold backed, they are sometimes used to hide a dipped or long back (although they often cover up the front as well by mistake). Some

exhibitors believe they can also soften a ride on a horse although, if they are too thick, the rider will appear to be perched high above the horse, which will probably give a rolling ride.

One of the most common mistakes in the bridle department is the use of too fine a bridle; they are often used by people who think that they will create a beautiful, refined picture. This usually works if the pony in question has the sweetest of heads, but this is often not the case and the plainer or bigger heads need to be covered more sensibly. It is common sense that a middleweight hunter will need a bridle made from wider leather than, say, a 13.2hh show pony. A leather plaited rein looks the part in the hunter type classes as well, although, needless to say, they should not be so long that they are considered dangerous.

I make no excuses for not going into detail about bits as I firmly believe that this is a great art, like feeding, and is basically up to the individual. The action of certain bits can have varying effects: a thin, twisted bridoon bit can pick up an animal's headcarriage whereas a pelham bit usually allows for a lower headcarriage. Many top showmen believe that a horse should not go into the ring until it is ready to take a double bridle and I must admit that horses in snaffle bridles do not look as dressed up in the ring. (In some BSPS classes, however, snaffle bridles are compulsory.) A useful compromise is to show your young horse in a broken pelham which acts in almost the same way as a jointed snaffle but looks like a double bridle. There has been much discussion as to whether three-year-old horses should be shown in hand in double bridles; those people against feel that it can damage a young mouth while the

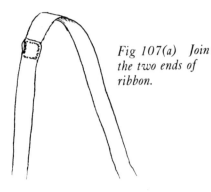

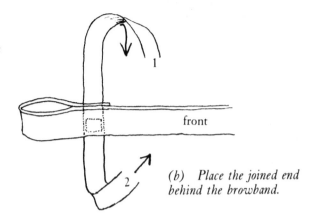

Fig 107(a) Join the two ends of ribbon.

front

(b) Place the joined end behind the browband.

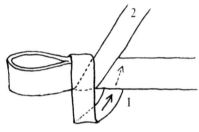

(c) Bring the lower piece, 2, upwards across the browband and the upper piece, 1, down over it (forming a triangle).

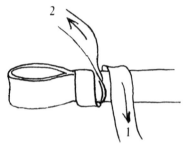

(d) Pull 2 back and wrap 1 round underneath 2.

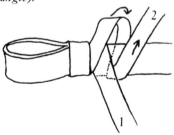

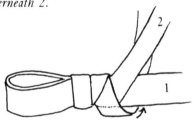

(e) Put 2 over top part of 1 and then wrap round browband under 1.

(f) Bring 1 over 2.

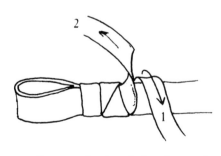

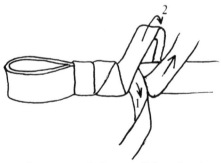

(g) Put 1 under 2 and then 2 over 1.

(h) Continue as before until browband is covered.

counter argument is that the handler has more control, which is better than jabbing in the mouth a horse that is wearing a snaffle bit, thus creating a dead mouth.

Whatever you choose, make sure it fits well and remember, if the animal is not comfortable he will not go well. In theory, if a horse has a good mouth, he should be able to take any bit, but in practice this varies from pony to pony and it is up to the producer to experiment for perfect results.

It is far better to make your own browbands than to buy them from the saddlers; in this way you can choose your own particular stable colours (the darker colour should always be at the top) and make a browband that suits the horse. Smaller, daintier pony heads obviously look better with narrower ones while for riding horses who may have plainer heads, use wide velvet on a wider browband. To be correct, hunters and hunter ponies should sport plain leather brow-

bands. The best way to learn to make a browband is to undo one first of all. Fig 107 will act as a guide. When you have finished covering most of the band, various decorative ends can be made by using belt stiffening (see Fig 108) but make sure these will not annoy the animal in the ring.

Just as there is a strict code of etiquette regarding dress in the show ring, so there are certain rules concerning tack in certain classes and exhibitors must be aware of these. For instance, no change of saddlery is allowed between phases in WHP classes. Exhibitors in these classes must also be careful not to offend judges by having, say, curb chains or martingales too tight, which may cause you to lose one or two marks with some judges.

Some exhibitors are campaigning for the use of brushing boots in the jumping phase of WHP classes but I, for one, would be totally against this owing to a personal experience when judging WHP classes in Dublin some years ago: brushing boots, which are allowed over there, were in some cases, deliberately used to hide cuts and blemishes.

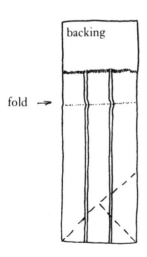

Fig 108(a) To make flags, stick required number of ribbon colours on to a stiff backing and shape ends as required.

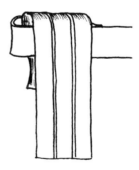

(b) Fold flags near the top allowing enough room to stick over the end of the browband. Stick into place.

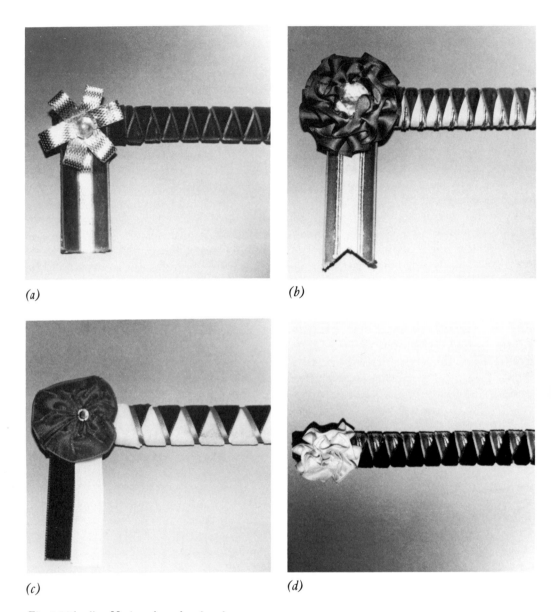

(a)

(b)

(c)

(d)

Fig 109(a-d)   Various browband ends.

Tack, like clothes, will last a long time if it is of good quality, cleaned regularly and maintained. Even though there are certain ground rules, exhibitors should use tack that enhances the appearance, improves way of going and, above all, suits the individual animal.

7 In the Ring

Showmanship – the art of making everything in the ring look so easy – is perfected with experience. Just as there are natural riders, so too there are natural showmen who glamorize their animals and manage to catch the judge's eye. Watch these people who have perfected their craft and learn how they make the most of the showring. An artist will sometimes make a Champion out of a good, though not necessarily outstanding, animal; but a bad showman will do little to help a potential Champion reach dizzy heights. Through being on the show circuit for a number of seasons, the top showman will also be aware of the capabilities of the judge, which is an important point.

It is amazing how many exhibitors trot into the ring and warm their animals up for a couple of circuits, probably because they have been wasting valuable time chatting in the collecting ring. All the working in should be done beforehand and any last minute checks should be dealt with in the collecting ring, whether this includes a quiet walk round, a limbering up at trot or pipe opener of a gallop. It is also amazing to see some trainers holding on to their exhibits at the ring entrance or even walking into the ring with them, letting them go like spinning tops once the judge has seen who they belong to; this should make no difference to a judge worth his salt – he is there to judge what he sees in front of him on the day, and not what appeared last week at the Royal or the last time he

judged the said exhibit. Instead, it is more polite for the animals to walk into the ring not too far away from the judge, with an even gap between each one. The experienced competitor will not go directly behind a better animal.

The walk of a show horse is very important as it is the first and the last pace a judge sees when in the ring. He should walk on a full, easy-going stride flowing over the ground (not into the ground), and from the shoulder (not the elbow) and with the hind legs well engaged, looking purposeful. A good walk denotes the ability to operate well at canter and, more particularly, at gallop.

A bad walk is when a horse or pony is behind the bridle and napping towards the pony behind or walking through the bridle (overwalking) with uneven choppy strides, or just simply jogging from side to side. Avoid the naughty animal in front of you, otherwise you run the risk of getting kicked or your own animal being encouraged to play up as well.

Usually, displays of bad manners take place directly in front of the judge. However, it can sometimes happen behind his back and a good steward will usually inform him of it although the problem here is that, unless the judge sees the misdemeanour for himself, it is extremely difficult for him to decide the seriousness of the offence and also to allow for any mitigating circumstances (for instance, a paper bag blowing underneath the animal). Horses should be asked to leave the ring if they are considered a danger to others. Good judges watch one side at a time so that all exhibits get an equal chance of being seen. Only when something can be heard or he suspects an animal is being naughty behind his back, because he may not have seen him for a while, does he look behind. The judges who follow certain animals around the ring, missing the majority of the class, should be reprimanded as all the exhibitors have paid their entry fee and deserve a fair crack of the whip.

Judges are often criticized for paying more attention to professionals' horses but, as one top judge said at a conference once, professionals cannot be expected to be infallible, but a judge will often give their horses a second look because he will expect them to know the requirements of the class. Taken further, the experienced exhibitor will know, over the years, what a particular judge prefers. Although we are all looking for the basic requirements, the finer details are a matter of personal opinion and judges attach a varying degree of importance to them. I can never understand why some exhibitors continually go under judges who do not like their animals; it is senseless, apart from being a costly venture. Another aspect of ringcraft is to make sure that, as a producer, you give your animal the best possible chance of succeeding – the show horse is totally reliant on your ability in this field.

Apart from keeping an eye on the judge (which does not mean continually glaring) in case he watches a different side, also observe the stewards who are there to assist the smooth running of the classes. If your walk has been correctly executed, the transition to trot (when asked to do so) should be automatic and smooth. It is important that the jockey rides on the correct diagonal otherwise his horse may look unbalanced and even lame (*see* Fig 110). In my opinion, the trot is the hallmark of the Champion show animal. There is nothing more disappointing when judging a class, than when your potential winner cannot get out of his own shadow at trot and I, personally, can forgive minor faults if an animal trots well. It can be strongly argued that Holly of Spring would possibly not have been as appealing, if she had not had such a natural and extravagant trot.

The trot should be balanced, rhythmic, two-time and smooth, with the animal tracking up well. Although the trot of the hunter, cob or WHP does not have to be as light and elegant as the hack or show pony, it should still be active and show a good length of low level stride – certainly not choppy or carriage-like nor too fast (landing on the heel) with the hind toes dragging behind. If your horse is naturally active, especially at this pace, he will be a delight to produce, whereas the horse with a poor trot will take more thoughtful producing.

As the pace moves up a gear, so the rider must be more on the ball. Aim to be in a clear space at the right time and not in a bunch. Novice or less experienced jockeys may, quite by accident (not on purpose one would hope) cover you up at the most vital moment, in front of the judge – so it pays to be aware of other riders' actions. To assist the judge, stewards at major shows insist that the rider shows off the horses' paces one behind the other, which at times is impractical when taking different lengths of stride into consideration.

There are a few ways to create more space, either by half-halting (claiming

Fig 110 Riding on the correct diagonal. When viewed from above on the right rein, as the outside shoulder is back, the rider is seated. When viewed from the side, when on the right rein, the rider is seated as the outside diagonal (indicated by the bandaged legs) is touching the ground.

your horse's attention) and collecting your animal, in this way gaining a few strides, or by going deeper into the corner or by finding another suitable opening in another part of the ring. You should not do this in front of the judge, interrupting his view, just as you should not keep circling incessantly, getting in everyone's way.

If a rider is not in control, this is usually revealed in canter. At times you would think that there was a special prize being awarded for the first one into canter, as a lot of exhibitors rush untidily into this at the first sign, (some people even canter before being asked with everyone following on, usually because their horses do not possess the ability to trot well). If

Fig 111   Aim to be in a clear space at the right time and not in a bunch.

this pace is prepared well (which usually entails waiting for a corner in the pony classes), the animal will maintain a correct shape and there will be less risk of striking off on the wrong leg, especially with the novice animal.

The canter should be collected yet going freely forward, with the hocks well under the horse and the shoulder coming off the ground as if in suspension. Too often we see animals behind the bit, not going forward and skipping on the spot, especially in hack classes, whereas in some other classes the horses are strong in the hand, running on through the bridle, completely unbalanced in anticipation of the gallop which is an extended variation of the canter, changing from three-time to four-time.

Depending on the class, you will be asked either to gallop on or to change the rein, in either case the rider must anticipate the steward's order. With the latter, map out well in advance where you are intending to trot and slip into left-rein

canter. If your mount really shines at this, do the change directly in front of the judge; if not, wait until you are on a strict left bend, particularly if cantering on the wrong leg is your tendency. Sometimes judges keep you trotting on the left rein, being conscious that some exhibits do not go equally as well on the opposite rein. Many hunter and cob exhibitors would like judges to request this more in their classes as they do in the pony and hack ones.

Changing the rein sometimes gives the judge a chance to see how the exhibits move towards and away from him for the first time – so if your horse trots wide behind or dishes in front, possibly because he trots too fast, either slow down the trot or start cantering much earlier before passing the judge. If you are riding a novice who does not like to meet others head on, allow enough space and lessen the odds of this happening by changing the rein very early.

Before galloping, the horse should be

on a longer canter stride, fully balanced on the corner so that he glides out of it fully stretched when in front of the judge. Do not take a full lap of the ring to find top gear – it will be too late and the judge, in his mind, will have dismissed you from top placings.

The gallop should show a lengthening of stride with the horse really using his shoulders as he lowers and glides along the ground with a great deal of athleticism; not showing a lot of knee action nor appearing to gallop into the ground. Some hunter competitors think that some judges place too much emphasis on the gallop when other paces and requirements are just as important in the hunting field – not everyone wants to be on board a flying machine all day. Pull up just as smoothly, not galloping up the back of the one in front of you in order to stop. Do not over-gallop if it is not necessary but if the judge asks for a second attempt, obey his wishes.

If your horse has remained balanced throughout the class, the downward transition into walk should be gradual, smooth, exact and maintained. Although the judge should be able to select a fair few at this stage, some judges like to see the class walk in a smaller circle, which is when the good steward will stop the scene from looking like a war dance with the judge in the middle. Many exhibitors at this stage (usually the ones who have let their animals go more sloppily throughout the class) allow their animals to amble along with looped reins in pleasant unconcern and often miss their opportunity when called into line.

When in line, remain attentive and make sure that your animal does not fall asleep, resting his hind leg or head on the floor, especially in hot weather. It is surprising how many judges cast a glance at the line-up during the class. Attentiveness is particularly important when leaving the line to commence your individual show, otherwise your horse will give the appearance of napping by showing unwillingness to leave the others.

This is your big chance to impress the judge and show how well trained your horse is. The clever exhibitor will keep the show short and sharp, showing off the horse to his best advantage and covering up his weaknesses. For instance, if your horse trots extravagantly perhaps contemplate an extra trot across the diagonal before cantering and include a good trot at the end of the show. If he does not, trot across the diagonal so the judge does not get a good sideways view, and particularly if he moves true instead. If your horse has a problem cantering on the right leg, design the show so that you canter on the left leg first. Similarly, if your horse twists when reining back, use the side of the ring as a guide, and perform the movement sideways on to the judge (and definitely not facing him), so there is no chance of his seeing that the movement is not straight. Remember not to gallop downhill – much better to extend uphill.

Although your show must represent some sort of pattern and cannot be too adventurous (unless in a Championship when it is deemed necessary), you may have to do something out of the ordinary to confuse the horse if he has a tendency to anticipate or if the unexpected happens, such as the course builder and fence stewards invading the ring in the middle of your show; and a flapping tent or a spectator's spooky umbrella need to be avoided.

Points to Remember

1. The closing stages of a show are the most memorable, so finish on a good note. There is more chance of a judge forgetting a mistake early on than at the end of an individual display. Do not give the impression of grinding to a halt either.

2. Use as much of the ring as you are allowed, especially with a novice, so that your transitions will be smooth, turns flowing and circles in the figure of eight or serpentine will be a good, even shape. Above all, do not rush – you are not competing for the world speed record. Choose good areas of going if the rings are rock hard or waterlogged and, if on a nervous horse, try to avoid the distraction at the ringside.

3. When reining back, keep the strides even, four backwards, four forwards with the horse on the bridle and listening to the leg. Do not rush back nor lunge forwards with an uneven number of strides.

4. Even though you may have a set routine, do exactly as the judge requests even if this is different from what you intended. He will not be able to make a comparison if all the exhibitors are doing something different.

5. When changing the rein in canter, make the transitions smooth, trotting for only a few strides before tripping into canter on the other rein. If you begin to change too early it can look untidy, especially if you trot for a long time as the smaller children do. If the change is made too late (ie. left until the horse is halfway round the second circle), it portrays to the judge that the horse is disobeying the rider's request.

6. Halt in front of the judge a reasonable distance away, not so close that he can see his reflection in your boots nor so far away that he would need field glasses to see you.

7. Make sure your horse halts squarely at the end of the show and the rider does not go over the top with the salute.

8. In a situation where the class is pulled into line in any order, as happens at Wembley, for instance, decide what suits your horse best regarding the judge's ride or your individual show: do you choose to go early while your horse is warmed up or let him settle more at the end of the line? Similarly, it may be advisable to keep on the horse in line until the last minute if he has a tendency to be cold-backed or fidgets in line when unmounted and vice versa.

9. Attention to detail is the formula for success. Keep jacket flaps over saddles and rein loops on the outside to help create a stylish and more accomplished look.

10. Look happy and confident, even if you are dying for the ground to swallow you up because things are going terribly wrong. A rider who had made the final judging at Wembley for the first time once described her emotions as being a combination of terror and delicious anticipation!

11. Cut your suit according to your cloth – for best results compete at your own level.

In some classes, the exhibits will be ridden by the judge in addition to or instead of an individual show. All show horses that are to be ridden by the judge must be 'judge-proof' and should go kindly for anyone (judges come in all shapes and sizes with a wide range of riding ability), as a class can be won or lost in this section. Asking riders of different ages and abilities to sit on your horse at home will help in this department. A show horse must have perfect manners and stand like a rock when the judge mounts and remain so until requested to move on.

If it is raining make sure that the saddle is dry for the judge, that the girth is tight enough and that the stirrup leathers are at roughly the correct length; it is advisable to check the measurements from a previously ridden horse if possible. If the saddle is not considered suitable by the judge, either because it or the stirrups are too small and leathers too short, he may refuse to ride the animal altogether.

When the judge approaches you at the riding stage (or at the start of an individual show), greet him with a cheery 'good morning' or 'afternoon' and do not get into a lengthy conversation with him. Particularly avoid discussing the horse's history, breeding or riding instructions. If the judge requires any further information he will ask, probably on returning the horse to you.

With regard to assisting the judge to mount, there is a happy medium between seeing him struggle and having a group of helpers fussing around. It may be that the judge will bring the horse out of line himself before mounting, with the help of only the steward. It is a good idea to do this yourself if you suspect the horse may be nappy leaving the line-up. Judges will soon become annoyed if horses are chased out of line when they are on board.

Many young show riders do not fully understand what makes a horse a good ride; they think that providing the horse has gone kindly, that will suffice. To ride a horse that is flowing, beautifully balanced (especially on the corners) and as soft

as an armchair is a pleasure indeed and is a product of correct and thorough schooling (which involves an interesting and varied work programme). During the ride, the judge will look for a response to the lightest of aids without any feeling of robotic anticipation on the part of the horse, who should wait for the command and not take the judge, especially when changing the rein. If a judge decides to ride on a long rein, the horse should still maintain a correct and light head carriage and not be all on the forehand or, worse still, stop. The transitions should be fluent with the horse relaxed, flexible and working forwards. The judge should not have to haul at the horse's head to obtain halt either, especially after galloping. A typical comment from a judge who receives a good ride is that he could have ridden that particular horse all day long.

Before presenting your horse for the in hand stage, make sure that all the sweat marks are brushed off and that the picture looks polished. A rosette can be won or lost depending on how well you perform and how much you impress the judge in the conformation phase.

Once remounted (and it is up to the rider to decide whether this should be straight away or at the last minute and whether the horse needs to be walked around the back of the line-up to get his back down), the class is usually sent out again in a small circle for final assessment, although the judge may well have an idea of the placings in his mind. It goes without saying that this is a very important time in the proceedings and the rider must concentrate and pay attention and present the horse at his very best. Some judges form a front line and dispense with this final stage altogether if they have already made their minds up; others will

Fig 112 Grooms busy at work in the ring next to the lake at the RIHS prior to the conformation phase.

Fig 113 Judge Elizabeth Mansfield gives an encouraging word to a young rider at the end of the line.

150

send the class into trot again – so be prepared.

Whether you are placed at the top or near the bottom of the line-up, accept the rosette with dignity. Even if you feel that you have been treated harshly, it will make up for the day when you may have been extremely lucky. After all, you put your animal under that judge on the day for his opinion, which was your choice in the first place and it is the conflict of opinion that makes showing so interesting. If approached politely, a judge will often explain the reasons for his placing of your horse. He may have noticed something of which you are unaware particularly if you see your animal through rose-coloured spectacles!

You must never be rude to a judge or fellow competitor otherwise you will soon gain a reputation for being a sore loser or bad sport, which no one likes. It is not the end of the world: there is always another day, another show and another judge. Opinions may differ, but everyone agrees that there is no room for bad manners — human or equine - in the small world of showing.

It is inevitable that some judges will become firm favourites as they consistently seem to like your type of animal and appreciate the way you present them while others, for the opposite reason, would be best avoided. Most exhibitors will often give a judge two or three chances before coming to the latter conclusion. On some occasions, even the judge is disappointed with his favourite pony because it has not performed or looked well on the day and is placed down the line.

8 Judging

Judging is based on personal opinion backed up by a sound knowledge of essential requirements applicable to each class including such criteria as movement, soundness, ride, conformation, type, manners, way of going and so on. Even though judges should all be looking for the same qualities, opinions do differ slightly since varying degrees of importance are attached to each quality. For instance, some judges will be influenced by the overall picture and presentation or the exceptional ride, while others will dismiss a horse with a weak hind leg. This is what makes the show ring a place of great speculation and interest.

Some judges become extremely nervous prior to judging a big show, but, although the task carries considerable responsibility, it should also be regarded as an enjoyable and challenging experience. Although exhibitors have entered their animal under you for your honest opinion, it is inevitable that some will not agree with your decisions, which should not bother the good judge who has the courage of his convictions.

When judging, it pays to keep an open mind at all times and, if you have missed a pony in the initial placings, do not be too proud to amend the situation and reward where necessary. I remember one of my 14.2 hh ponies at one stage standing twenty-third at the BSPS Welsh Championships, but ending up Champion after the judge admitted that he had missed the pony at the beginning.

Being very much involved in the showing world as a council member, judge and an exhibitor, I often find that I am judging animals that belong to close friends, which does not bother me providing rules are not being broken. In fact, because many exhibitors expect me to lean towards fellow professionals or form animals, I fall over backwards to give everyone an equal chance and if friends cannot cope with being down the line (if that is what they deserve), then they are not, in my opinion, true friends.

At a judges' assessment day a few years ago, one of my co-examiners asked the candidates a question which to my mind did not have an obvious answer: if you had two animals of equal merit and you could not decide which one should stand above the other, one was owned by a close friend and the other by a complete stranger, what would you do? The majority wanted to say that they would put up the friend's pony but, in the circumstances, chose the other option instead, which was interesting but equally unfair. In this situation, I think the only possible solution is to find a way to separate them even if it is by choosing the one you would prefer to take home. In the past, I have seen judges awarding two first prizes which does seem to be taking the easy way out.

As you can see, judging is not as easy and straightforward as it may appear from the ringside and it is only when you have officiated from the middle of the ring that you begin to appreciate the difference.

Observations when Judging

Even though the best judges are those who conduct their classes in a relaxed and friendly manner, they should not be seen to be familiar with certain competitors who are perhaps close friends because it looks bad to the other exhibitors. The BSHC & RHA recommend that 'It is insufficient to be merely impartial; judges must also be seen to be impartial.'

Do not ask the breeding of exhibits until the end of the class in case you may have the slightest connection with it. For example, it may be by your stallion or related to something you have for sale at home.

Although, with the increasing costs of entry fees, all competitors' horses should be ridden or allowed to give a show, this should not be at the expense of allowing sufficient time to concentrate on the top placings, which do require accurate judging.

As a member of a society's panel, judges should be familiar with the rules, requirements and proceedings of the showing classes (including awarding special rosettes). I often carry the relevant rule book and schedule (not a catalogue!) of the show with me when judging, just in case an unusual situation arises which requires reference to the rule book.

The class is not finished until the steward dismisses the line-up, before which time the judge is entitled to remove a rosette from any prize-winner displaying bad manners in the line-up so, technically, the class is not actually won when the rider has the rosette in his hand. With reference to manners, if a judge considers an exhibit to be ill-mannered he is within his rights to ask the exhibit to retire.

Another much discussed point is when you should allow late arrivals into the class. Depending on the circumstances, I would normally allow a late comer into the ring providing the class had not started cantering (or, in the case of in hand classes, before the initial pulling into line) because you can see how it walks and trots in company later in the proceedings. I would expect riders to acknowledge the steward or judge in this situation and not just sneak into the ring unannounced. Similarly, exhibitors who leave the ring prematurely without the consent of the judge should, in my book, be reported to the relevant societies, as it is the height of bad manners – like taking away your bat and ball because you are not winning the game.

Judges should also never arrive late for the classes – some even forget to arrive at all. If ever you are unable to fulfil a judging appointment, for whatever reason, inform the secretary as soon as possible. At one show this year, a distraught show secretary only found a replacement judge for her RIHS qualifying classes after making twenty-three phone calls. Once you have agreed to judge at a show (a commitment which should be treated as an honour), that should stand – you must never give backword (which some judges have actually done) even if a better judging invitation for the same day arrives later. It is like being invited out for dinner and then letting the hostess down at the last minute because you have been asked out by others who will give you a better meal.

No judge should ever consider putting an unbeaten Champion show horse down the line in order to make a name for himself and gain publicity.

Co-judging can be fun especially if your ideas are compatible with each other. If, on the other hand, there is a strong conflict of ideas, do not necessarily back down all the time, even to a senior judge; the only profitable action open to you instead, is to compromise on the placings. I personally prefer to see co-judges together all the time otherwise, if split up (as they are at Wembley), there can be some surprise results even from the judges point of view!

Good stewards are few and far between. If you are lumbered with a noisy busybody who gives you every horse's history, it is kinder in the long run to tell him to shut up. Never be seen to be laughing and joking with your steward while a competitor is doing an individual display – it could be misinterpreted and assumed that you are laughing at the competitor.

If one looks at the letters page in past issues of the horsy press, one can clearly see that complaints about judges and judging are old hat and not a modern-day occurrence. If exhibitors, or for that matter judges, feel they have a justifiable complaint, most societies have an efficient complaints procedure to deal with it. All too often, people are ready to question a judge's integrity. It is a small world and, without a great deal of effort, it is so easy to make a connection between an exhibitor or a judge and consequently, you often hear of a placing being 'fixed'.

Even though new judges are appointed annually, it is the smaller shows who usually take the plunge and invite them to officiate, rather than the big ones who pick the same old faces on whom they believe they can rely. Show secretaries should always offer judges travelling expenses (and accommodation if neces-sary) and make sure that a good lunch is provided (not an apple and a chocolate biscuit). Judging, even if no riding is involved, can be very tiring. With this in mind, secretaries should not overwork a judge, running the risk of his losing concentration.

If judging a mixed Championship such as a Supreme or Mountain and Moorland one – make sure you know what each exhibit represents. Sometimes one hears of judges withholding a first prize or a qualification because he considers the class to be below the standard. This is unfair on the exhibitors who have supported the show and they should not be penalized for having had the good fortune to be in the right place at the right time.

As interest in judges' preferences and judging methods increases, many exhibitors would like to see more showing classes being judged on a points system, similar to Wembley and WHP classes. I believe, however, that although points systems using skating marks include the spectators more and provide a refreshing alternative to normal judging, not all judges can cope with them and find difficulty in putting their thoughts into numbers. Apart from this, adding points is very time consuming and relies heavily on a competent steward. After all, the judging process is a private affair and should not be an exercise in mental arithmetic. Instead, I wish judges would make more notes, especially when confronted with huge classes.

Although a few words of encouragement will not go amiss and are often appreciated, judges must take care what they say to competitors, especially children, in case it is misconstrued.

Ride judges should not abuse their

Fig 114 Lady Benton Jones referring to her notes while judging the 13.2hh show pony class at Kent County Show in 1988.

privileged position when judging but treat competitors' horses as they would their own, giving them time to settle and riding them with tact and sympathy. If most of the horses go badly for a judge, it reflects harshly on his ability. A bad judge will expect all horses to adjust to his style of riding rather than the other way round.

An old horseman once said that the mark of an excellent judge was one who was able to discover a new Champion on its debut appearance amongst an array of established star performers.

A water-tight system of obtaining new judges has yet to be found, although the present-day system of holding assessment days, followed by a probationary scheme works well in most cases and does at least encourage new blood unlike the closed-shop attitude of the past. A common problem is that many senior judges from other panels are too proud to consider going on to a probationary panel, which is unfortunate as, in many cases, these are the people we need. Sadly, many of the successful candidates are sometimes the best of a mediocre group of people who have never bred or owned anything like they are judging. When appointing new judges, selectors must be careful to avoid the grace and favour

155

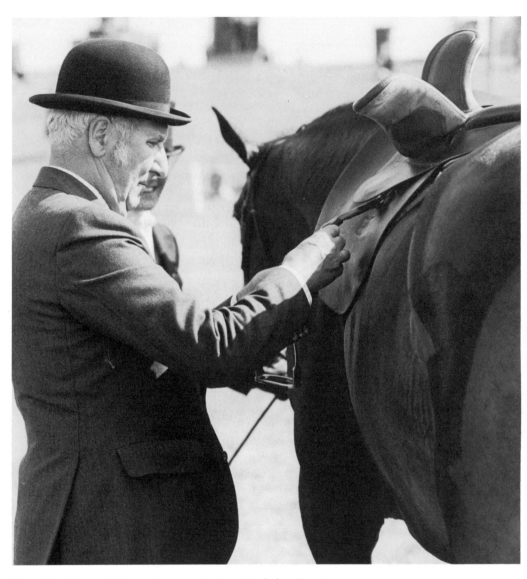

Fig 115 Dennis Colton, adjusting the length of the stirrup
leather for the judge in a ladies' hunter class.

situation of show ring politics; they must
choose only those people who are capable
of judging well, and often under pressure,
the enormous classes of valuable show
animals.

When a probationary judge accom-
panies me at a show, I do not expect to
agree with his placings or he with mine as
no two judges totally agree. However, I
will only write a favourable report if I feel
that in time I would, as an exhibitor, be
happy to take my own animals under this
person for a fair hearing. Senior judges
have a responsibility to the governing
society and members to ensure that the
high standard of judging is maintained.

9 Expert Opinions

I have always been interested in listening to other peoples' opinions to see how they match or differ from my own, primarily in order to increase my knowledge since I am a great believer in the fact that, with show animals that are all different to produce, you will never stop learning. Consequently, I have asked several top people who are specialists in their fields to give their own personal views on various aspects of showing to help answer the question so often heard: 'What are the judges looking for?'. Whereas in racing, the end result is reached by the first one past the winning post, in showing it is far more complicated in that the results are based purely on the opinion of the judge in question on that day and how you the producer and/or exhibitor have influenced that opinion.

The Role of a Show Secretary by Ben Harwood

From an early age, Ben Harwood has been connected with shows as an exhibitor, judge and organizer in a voluntary capacity. In 1950, he was appointed chairman of the Darwen Agricultural Society, a post that was previously held by his late father. When his family business was sold in the early 1970s, he approached the Royal Lancashire Agricultural Society (when they were moving their show ground from Blackpool to Ribby Hall, Wrea Green) and asked if they required any assistance. At the time, no help was required but a month or so later in June 1972, their secretary phoned and asked if he would be willing to assist them for a few days.

Those few days lasted some fifteen years. He was made assistant secretary in May 1973, took over as secretary in June 1974 and continued until he retired in March 1987. What had started as a hobby became his full-time occupation and he became one of the key figures in the gradual recovery of the Society's fortunes.

During its many ups and downs, I thoroughly enjoyed my association with the RLAS.

During the period I was secretary, I not only had responsibility for the Annual Show organization but the additional experience of planning two new showgrounds at Witton Country Park, Blackburn and at Aintree Racecourse.

It is impossible for the secretary of a larger society to do everything on his own – he is just one of a team – and for all the years I was secretary of the RLAS, I was most fortunate in having the support of an excellent council and show committee, assisted by most reliable stewards and a most conscientious ground foreman.

A question I have been asked on many occasions is, when does the show planning commence? What many may not realize is that some things have to be arranged for next year's show before the current show has been held. No two shows are the same with their organization, but all have the same end product and the hope of being favoured with good weather. With the introduction of modern technology such as computers, word processors, photo-copiers and electronic typewriters, many changes have been made during the last decade in show organization, especially for the larger societies.

Following the annual show, my first priority was to check the marked catalogue which the awards senior steward had prepared for me against the award slips from the judges' books, and then to complete various breed society result forms and send them along with a 'marked catalogue' for their particular section. This is quite a task and must be done with urgency and without error.

Next comes the preparation of the award statements, cheques for all the lucky prize-winners, the settlement of all the accounts from creditors and the preparation of draft accounts ready for the first council meeting after the show, when council members always want to know if the show was a financial success. During my days as secretary, prize money and all accounts received were paid before taking my holidays in early September.

A few days after sending prize money cheques, one or two letters were sometimes received from very irate exhibitors complaining that prize money received was incorrect or that some prize money had not been included. On investigation,

it was usually found that an incorrect number had been entered on the judge's book result sheet and so I cannot stress enough the importance for stewards to enter the results without error and at the same time check that the exhibitor is wearing the correct number for the class.

Another urgent post-show job is to check trophy results and enter up the names of the current winners on the trophy record register, making special note of whether the trophy has been taken away by the winner and a signed receipt obtained. Nothing is more annoying to an exhibitor than to be asked to return the trophy when in fact they did not take it. Trophies are a nightmare to all show secretaries and, from discussions with other secretaries at their annual conferences, all have the same problems and as far as I am aware, a foolproof solution on trophies has yet to be found.

As early as possible after the show, section committee meetings are arranged when members discuss and agree on the section classification, judges, prize money and entry fees for the next show, following which invitations to the first choice of judges are sent without delay. Arranging judges can drag on for months and I have known times when the printing of the schedule has been delayed, awaiting the name of a judge. Some judges can be slow in replying: to wait a month and then get a refusal has often happened. To overcome this, an invitation can be worded to the effect that if a reply is not received by a certain date, it will be assumed that the judge is unable to accept and another judge would then be invited.

The first document to be produced for the following year's show was the trade stand application form, together with their rules and regulations and these were usually sent out in November. Other urgent items were to request estimates for various show requirements such as marquees, public address systems, toilets, security and also to request tenders for catering, bars, mobile snacks and ice cream. A further urgent priority is to make enquiries about the availability and cost of main ring attractions, ready for approval by the show committee.

In recent years sponsorship has become an essential part of any show and many would not be able to continue in their present form without it, so potential sponsors must be approached early otherwise their allotted sum for their current year may already have been allocated. All shows owe a great debt of gratitude to their sponsors and so they should be offered the very best of hospitality.

Many exhibitors wonder why entries have to close so early and there are several reasons for this. Entry closing dates have to be staggered to spread the work load and the sections requiring the most entering up are normally done first. Also, the catalogue printer wants the largest sections first and, finally, until entries have closed and the final number of entries for main ring classes is known, it is impossible to work out an accurate main ring timetable. It is mainly the shows with a printed catalogue of entries who have to have an early closing date and this is very often a thorny problem with many exhibitors. All kinds of excuses are made in the hope that late entries will be accepted but, having been an exhibitor for many years, I usually had no problem in knowing which excuses were genuine (having made many of the same excuses myself in the past). Here again, entry

procedure varies from show to show but so far as I was concerned, once the decision not to accept further entries was made, this decision was strictly adhered to no matter who the exhibitor was. From experience, it was usually found that anyone who had had their entries returned because of lateness were very often the first to enter the following year.

Still on the subject of entries, there are many ways in which an exhibitor can assist a show secretary and his staff. Most shows will automatically send a schedule to all who exhibited at their previous show but do not take this for granted and, if you have not received one send for one in plenty of time. Always state the section that you require, as a show can have a separate schedule for each section of the show. At the same time, ask for the number of entry forms required. To ask for just a horse schedule is not always sufficient; there can be several horse schedules, so state the classes for which a schedule is required.

Some schedules will give you details of the exhibitor and vehicle passes to which you are entitled, so check that your allocation is sufficient and, if not, send for more. This is far better than having an argument with the gateman on show day.

Fill in your entry form clearly. Having to try and decipher bad writing can waste considerable time and it has been known for some exhibitors to become quite annoyed if the names or the breeding of their animals have been printed incorrectly in the catalogue. Having completed your entry form, make a note of the classes and the animals which you have entered, before sending it with your entry fees. Enclose a S.A.E. if you require an acknowledgement. By the time that your exhibitor's tickets are sent, entries

Fig 116   Security in the stable area at many major shows
is a problem, especially as most of these animals are
liable to dope testing.

will have closed and requesting an acknowledgement gives you time to check that you have not made any errors; if you have, there will still be time to contact the secretary before entries go to print. Nothing can be more infuriatating than to receive a phone call (just prior to the show when life is becoming really hectic) from an exhibitor asking what animals have been entered.

Send entries in well before the closing date and, should extra entry forms be required, ask for more in good time. Making out your own on a plain piece of paper is not always adequate since it may not adapt to the show entry system. Consequently, time has to be spent rewriting your entire entry. Some shows also require a separate entry form for each exhibitor, so please check that you have sufficient for your requirements well in advance. Most of my headaches with entries came from the owners of livery yards who were entering animals for several owners and our system of entries

would not function correctly without a separate form for each exhibitor. In my early days, I would complete additional forms myself, but this became far too time consuming and so I started to return entries with the additional blank forms. Many of the top livery yards showing today have had entries returned by me. What their entries were like for other shows, I do not know, but I did get the majority to comply with my system.

Many exhibitors hate having to stay after their classes for the Grand Parade but this is unavoidable. For the majority of the general public, the Grand Parade is the main highlight of the show so please do organize yourself to have sufficient handlers for the animals to be paraded.

When next doing your entries, please have a thought for the many hard-working show secretaries and bear in mind some of the points I have raised. Another showing season will soon be upon us and the very best of luck to you all.

The Role of the Steward by Dennis Colton

Dennis Colton is one of the many hard-working stewards but is probably the best known at both the RIHS and The Horse of the Year Show.

Every successful show is the result of good team-work. The organizing committee are the hub of the wheel. They organize the whole show, decide the classes and formulate the schedule. The secretariat are the pivot on which the whole thing revolves. The officials, commentators and stewards are the spokes and rims of the wheel that carries the whole thing along. It is the attitude and pleasant demeanour of the gate officials and car park attendants, the first people that anyone attending the show will meet, who set the tone for the day. It is the commentators who inform, instruct and create the atmosphere of the show itself and who, together with the stewards, run the various rings, carry on the work started by the organizing committee and who make or break the success of the whole event. However superb the venue and facilities, the main criterion is the sport and the competitors who present that sport to the paying public.

A show steward has responsibilities in four different areas. The first is to the show that appointed him to the job: he must ensure that his ring is run smoothly, without fuss or aggravation and, most important, in strict accordance with the schedule formulated by the organizing committee. Someone once said that laws are made for the guidance of the wise and the compliance of the foolish. This certainly cannot apply to the schedule, which is absolutely sacrosanct as far as the ring steward is concerned.

The second of the steward's responsibilities is to the breed or show society for which the show is acting as agent, be it HIS, BSPS, Hack, Cob and Riding Horse or any other. It is the steward's function to ensure that the class is judged in accordance with that society's rules and regulations and the steward must know those rules just as well as the judge. He or she should carry a copy of the rules on his clipboard and be able to produce them in moments of crisis, if required.

The third duty is to the competitor, to ensure that everyone, regardless of who he is, gets the same fair crack of the whip. The competitor must know that the class is being judged in strict accordance with the conditions of the schedule, of which they have indicated their acceptance by their attendance.

Last, and by no means least, the steward has a duty to the public who have paid to attend to see as well-presented a spectacle as possible with each section of the class presented to them in accordance with regulations (which the majority of the spectators know as well as anyone in the ring). Justice to the spectators must be seen to be done and judgement passed fairly and without contention. Each of these responsibilities are of equal importance and the ring steward is the servant of them all.

He should maintain a proper demeanour at all times. He should be courteous, helpful, patient and tolerant of other people's failings. He should never lose his temper with an exhibitor or get into an argument, nor should he niggle or hassle people or throw his weight around unnecessarily. Exhibitors are under enough pressure already to give of their best. They are there to enjoy the day and the competition or, as in the case of the professional showman, to earn their living. They are not there to be shouted at by some badge-bedecked bowler-hatted moron with a loud voice and suit to match. It is authority overtly implied and covertly applied which epitomizes the efficient steward's dealings with competitors in his ring.

To the steward, the ring in his charge is all-important. It must run smoothly and to time. As a steward, you should always get to the showground early. Invariably, it is before the class starts that the problems are most likely to occur and it is a good thing if you are there to help deal with them. Always be well turned out: you owe it to the show and to the competitors. Apart from your clip-board which will contain the schedule, programme of events and entries, rules of the society (whose classes are being judged), judge's books and spare sheets of paper, you will need a pencil (since most ball-point pens do not write in the rain), ballpoint pens (two colours, red and black), a tape measure to measure the length of whips or canes, etc., a clean, folded handkerchief in case of accidents and a pocket knife.

Make your mark in good time with the secretariat. They will put you in the picture if there are likely to be any problems or objections and give you time to make your dispositions accordingly. Collect your entry sheets and judge's books and ascertain how many rosettes you can award, whether there are any 'specials' and whether any sponsors will be presenting, and so on.

Liaise closely with your commentator and collecting-ring steward. They are of equal importance in the show team. It is the commentator who creates the atmosphere of the class and who keeps the public informed. The duties of the collecting-ring steward are many and varied. He must keep the horse-box lines informed of how much time they have before the next class, check off the numbers of entries and ensure that the riding in is carried out safely and in the correct tack. They will, in the absence of the stipendary steward, ensure that practice fences are built, and jumped, in accordance with regulations, and that no illegal obstacles or equipment is used. In jumping classes, the collecting-ring steward certainly earns his lunch.

Having set up contact with your colleagues and found out what the arrangements are regarding first aid and the veterinary surgeons, check to see that your ring is clear of hazards and capable of complete closure. You can now make your mark with your judge.

The relationship between the judge and the ring steward is all-important. The judge has a difficult job to do in that, in a class of twenty competitors, he can only please one person – the one at the top of the line – and all the competitors know before the class started that they should be there by divine right anyway. In every show class he judges, the judge puts his reputation at stake and it is the steward's function to make the judge's job as smooth and trouble-free as he can. The steward is the servant of the judge and is their contact intermediary between him and the competitors. It is the steward who will pass on the judge's instructions to the exhibitors for their compliance and no one is allowed to have contact with the judge once the class has commenced. Never be familiar with your judge: in front of the exhibitors, judges are always Sir or Madam, no matter how well you know them personally. Be attentive without being obtrusive, never block the judge's view of the exhibits. Stand behind, a couple of yards away, and let him know you are there. Keep him in the picture if anything happens behind his back but never offer an opinion. To the public and exhibitors alike, it must appear that the judge is in sole charge of the ring and that all orders and instructions eminate from them. Nothing must happen in the judging of the class without the consent of the judge.

Once the class comes into the ring, it is the steward's function to check the numbers against the list of entries and to see that dress and tack are in accordance with the regulations. Never hurry your judge during the preliminary phase. Once the judge has decided to call in his preliminary line-up, be positive in your signal to the competitors called. If you are getting behind your judge in bringing the exhibitors in, call a check. There is nothing worse than having to reshuffle a line after you have made a mistake and called in the wrong animal. To the exhibitor and spectator, it does not mean the steward has fallen down on the job; it means the judge cannot make up his mind. Always let the judge know when your front line is complete. If I can avoid it, and there is room, I will not have a second row but make one long line down the ring leaving a gap between, say, the first twelve and the remainder. The second row can be a very lonely place and the wind of good opinion blows very cold in that area.

Never, ever ignore those at the end of the line. They are equally important as those at the top. They have paid the same entry money as the others and, if you treat them with scant courtesy, you are a fool and a liability to the sport.

The judge's ride is all-important and should, more than anything, assist him in arriving at the correct result. Professional show exhibitors are past masters at making a silk purse out of a sow's ear while you watch – this is why the top show riders are so good at their job. Personally, in ridden classes where there is a set show, I would like to see the judge ride first and then say, with confidence, which animals they would like to see an individual show from and which ones stripped. At least the less successful exhibitor can say that his animal had been ridden by the judge, even if they are subsequently required to do an individual show in twos or threes.

In ridden show pony classes, some people say that the set or specified show is destroying the incentive of the exhibitor, but I do not agree. In allowing a 'DIY' or unrestricted show things can only go from bad to worse as a flustered child endeavours to ride a pre-programmed pony through a show that has gone wrong from the outset. At all times, put children at their ease. Explain carefully to every child what they are required to do, repeat it if necessary, never hurry them and, when they get back into line, tell them how good they were. A set show not only saves time but gives the viewing public the opportunity of comparing like with like, by knowing what to look for in every show forward.

Once the ride and show phases are completed, the class enters its penultimate phase: the run up in hand or conformation. As a rule of thumb, a class with, say, fifteen competitors in line should be completed, presentation and all, in twenty minutes and it is now that you warn the collecting ring to start giving the fifteen-minute call to the next class.

As soon as the last animal has completed his show or the judge has stepped off the last exhibit to be ridden, the first two for the conformation section should be standing out in front of the main spectator area. Always send them out side by side, but a little way apart. It gives the audience the chance of comparing one with the other and the judge has only to turn round to see the next, once he has finished with the first. As soon as the first horse trots away, the third in line is sent forward to take his place.

As the class comes to its end, warn the collecting ring to call up the next class, and the commentator to prepare his announcements. Once the winning line is formed, make up the results card, without alterations of any kind, and get the judge to sign it before sending it off to the secretariat. The presentation is always important so make sure that the press photographer has a clear picture of the winner and the sponsor (if any), unimpeded by rosette ladies, course builders and so on. Thank the judge and sponsor for their courtesy and escort them from the ring.

What happens when you have to wave the red card? This is never pleasant but it does happen.

Be generous with late arrivals especially when it is the first class of the day. There could be traffic problems getting into the showground or many other valid reasons for lateness. Be tolerant and, always with the judge's permission, call them into the ring for as long as you can.

Once the judge has instructed you to call the first exhibit into the preliminary line-up, the class is definitely closed.

Showing is all about presentation and correct turn-out is all part of that show. Exhibitors and attendants owe it to the show and the public to be properly turned out. If the schedule specifies a requisite dress for grooms and attendants, it must be complied with and I will ask those not properly dressed to leave the ring to get the proper attire, without any reference to the judge. Otherwise, exhibitors can only be asked to leave with the judge's express consent. Manners are all-important in showing classes, in both the riders and their exhibits. If, during the judging of a class, a horse or pony kicks out at another, tries to unseat his rider or behaves to the detriment of the rest of the class, I will bring that exhibit's behaviour to the notice of the judge and, at their direction, request the exhibitor to leave the ring.

If, in the opinion of the judge, there is some doubt respecting the soundness of an exhibit and a veterinary surgeon is available, the exhibit should be taken out of the ring by the steward for the veterinary surgeon to inspect. If the vet is satisfied that the horse is sound, then, with the judge's permission only, he should be allowed back into the ring. If the judge does not want him back, he must remain out, but this seldom happens. If no veterinary surgeon is available, the judge's decision is final.

If, in pony classes, a child is thrown by a misbehaving animal, do not assist the child to remount. Pony classes are all about mannered ponies and, if an exhibit has shown himself to be unmannerly, you are putting that child in danger if you allow him to remount. With the permission of the judge, you should run up the stirrup irons, take the rein over the pony's head and lead the pony out of the ring yourself to show to the spectators that, in the opinion of the judge, the pony is dangerous and not fit to be ridden by a child.

Do not become involved in objections or in giving opinions on occurrences. The schedule lays down the procedure for making objections and this must be adhered to at all times.

A good ring steward makes a show, a bad steward can ruin it for exhibitors and spectators alike. The ideal ring steward has the tact of a diplomat, the charity and forbearance of a saint and the ability to absorb punishment of a practising masochist, but it can be great fun and you meet lovely people.

Judging by Donald Owen

Donald Owen came from a non-horsy background, but had a natural eye for a horse ('something you are born with and improves with experience'). This stood him in good stead when he started his business in 1956 and, over the years, became a leading producer and rider of successful show horses and most sought after judge of hacks, cobs and ponies, until he retired owing to ill-health.

He bought his first horse (Mr Sponge) from the late Tommy Grantham of Stroller fame after selling a litter of pigs for £130: Mr Sponge later finished sixth in the working hunter class at Harringay, then the home of The Horse of the Year Show, after Donald's aunt lent him 30/- for the entry fee and £7.00 for the hire of the horse-box.

'I have never forgotten the thrill of winning that first London rosette, and this is something which has remained at the back of my mind when judging other people'. One of the reasons he was such a popular judge was that he would often explain to exhibitors why they were placed in a certain order and commanded their respect because he was so pleasant and helpful.

Donald has produced many champions but perhaps one of his yard's best advertisements was when Bow Bells, who won the Small Hack title at Wembley with Donald in 1961, also won the year after, this time produced by an amateur owner.

I often felt honoured that so many people would bring good animals under me for my opinion, a situation I never abused, believing that judges should treat competitors' animals as they would their own. Sporting Rights, one of my best horses, became very sharp and ringcrafty because the judges would often over-gallop him as he was such a wonderful ride. It was also with this horse that I learnt a very valuable lesson in ringcraft. At Wembley in 1968, I had won both the lightweight class with New Moon and the middleweight class with Sporting Rights, whom I elected to ride in the Championship as he was the fancied horse. In my over-confidence, I allowed David Tatlow (who was riding State Visit, the heavyweight winner) to catch me napping and, consequently, he out-galloped me and duly won the title.

If horses have natural ability, which is produced in the right way, the picture will automatically come together. I bought a hack called Blue Link who had a reputation, from the West Country during the season. I took her home and returned with her to the area the week after (at the Castle Cary Show) and won the Hack Championship, which proves this theory.

When I judged horses, I expected to enjoy riding them. After all that is what ridden horses are for and if it was an extremely good class, the ride took priority over everything. One of the best rides I have ever sat on was my top lightweight hunter Daddy's Choice who was not perfection on four legs, but was untouchable when going because he loved the job and went well for the judge, which is also another reason why this horse was practically unbeaten in ladies' hunter classes.

When riding, I liked horses that would respect the leg, bend correctly on both reins and were beautifully balanced. Sometimes, I am left cold when watching modern-day showing classes, as the majority of horses go so badly, especially in their individual show which is basic-ally due to lack of knowledge with their production.

I am a great believer in horses going in a straight line and used to lead from both sides, particularly from the offside if the horse had been shown in hand. Newton Belle was an exception in that she was shown successfully in hand and also under saddle, being a prolific winner of small hunter classes. However Herb of Grace was another story: although suc-cessful as a middleweight hunter, win-ning the RIHS (after which he was retired to the hunting field), he hated the showing job as he was extensively shown in hand since a foal, which made him a soured ridden horse.

In many ways, I would prefer a horse that has not been shown at all. If I like a horse I will buy him, regardless of pre-vious results.

As a judge you should not be influen-ced by the well-known faces in the ring or the on-form animal's previous results, but judge on the day as you see the class. When I first started, as an unknown, I took on the professionals and beat some of them, often with young horses who had no, or very little, previous form. A show horse should be like a person on the stage; he should have natural elegance and presence and say 'look at me'. With such a horse, you can sometimes get away with murder.

I prefer a Thoroughbred horse above all and like to see a good hind leg (which is where the power comes from). Usual-ly, a horse that stands correctly without being put there, often turns out to be the most naturally balanced ride. When looking at horses, I would often listen to the way that they trotted on a hard sur-face, with my back turned away.

Judges should learn to be adaptable. In certain circumstances, exuberance up to a point can be forgiven from an outstand-ing finely tuned show exhibit, often having to cope with today's show ring distractions. After all, you are judging a show horse not a police horse, and I loathe to see dull horses with their heads on the floor in the show ring because they have been worked excessively.

166

Whereas some producers would advocate schooling a hack differently to a hunter, I have always schooled my horses in the same way. My hunters used to go like hacks (very light in their mouths and carrying their heads in the correct position) because they were schooled correctly. I could see no justification in allowing a heavyweight hunter to pull a judge's arms out just because he was not a hack. In my view, you either school them properly or you do not, which I believe is why I had so much success with young horses that did not enter the ring until they were fully ready. I expected them to be on their way to being ready in six months, otherwise I often found they never would be at all. I produced and rode Feudal Knight to win the Hack of the Year title when he was a four year old.

As a judge, I have had to ride in some very uncomfortable saddles. I am not a fan of the modern dressage-type saddle which does not allow you to be close to the horse like the traditional Owen and, while on the subject of tack, some of the browbands seen on today's hacks and ponies belong more to fancy dress than to the show ring!

Although mostly involved with horses, one of my favourite pastimes was judging children's ponies because they were so interesting and proved such a challenge. The production in pony classes is so much higher and the children are so marvellous that one really had to concentrate to sort them out, almost like judging the hunters at Dublin. I strongly advise judges to jot down the odd number when confronted with large classes – how else do you remember which one of the six greys in the bunch caught your eye? If, by chance, you miss a good pony or one does a particularly good show, there is no reason why you should not ask your steward to move him up the line during the class rather than run the risk of forgetting him, because of his initial placing. However, I do not agree with pulling ponies in to line in reverse order, even though it may assist the judge, since I believe that this is most unfair on the children involved.

An older pony would not worry me providing that he goes about his job; but displays of bad manners do worry me and must be penalized accordingly, although a bigger pony, capably ridden, can get away with a little more. I am disgusted at dealers who sell difficult ponies to unsuspecting parents, as the children can easily get hurt.

If you have basic knowledge and know what you like and dislike, the judging process becomes easy and fun. However, if you do not know what to look for and how to assess what you see, the situation can become a nightmare, in which you become easily confused, having found faults with all of them.

These days judging on the whole leaves a lot to be desired and I cannot see how judges, on some days, can justify their placings. Perhaps they do not have the courage of their convictions, which is a must if one is to be a successful judge.

Hacks by John Keen

Although John Keen is better known as a producer of show hacks, he has enjoyed success in other disciplines of equestrianism, having competed in the King George V Gold Cup and European Eventing Championships, as well as breeding successful competition animals such as Working Hunter Pony of the Year Sefton Tony of Alderbourne and Wild Life, one of Michael Whittaker's first Grade A horses who was by Evening Trial out of a mare saved from slaughter. He even learned how to ride side-saddle so that he could school Mirage for Mrs Mackintosh, which won the ladies' class at Royal Windsor, the Royal International and Richmond Royal.

At one time, he also produced beauty queens. This came about when a friend entered a beauty competition with a skiing holiday as first prize. Produced by John, the friend won the competition. Looking back, he says that there were many similarities to showing: conformation faults were covered up with clever use of costumes (like tack on a show animal) and some girls who were very ordinary could look like a million dollars on the catwalk because they had presence (just as a Champion in the show ring does).

He enjoys the challenge of a difficult horse. In many ways, an easy one would be boring, which is just as well, as the horses within the price bracket that he could afford have in the most part been 'specialist horses'. His greatest joy is to have a horse perform so that one has made the seemingly impossible, possible and one has a horse that enjoys working with and for you.

A favourite horse is the star of the moment and ideally, you would wish for a stable full of stars so that there is no particular favourite. Having said that, Formidable would rate as one of the best, as he presented a tremendous challenge and Oakley Blowing Bubbles (twice Small Hack of the Year) was a star rather than an actor, because he would rise to the occasion. He had a very good temperament and, as the late Count Robert Orssich said, 'action to burn'.

When buying a hack, I first look for a horse who catches my attention (preferably a Thoroughbred) and one with presence. The Champion has it in abundance, although it is true to say that some of this can be cultivated with production. Then I look for the chinks in the china

such as curbs, spavins, twisted feet which usually result in my going no further with the potential purchase.

When judging, if there were two horses of equal merit regarding soundness, ride and manners, one of which was classic when standing still and the other when on the move, I would prefer the latter. Although in theory, the best put-together horse should be a good mover and vice versa, this does not always follow in practice, as on occasions a horse with poor conformation can often move very well.

In the ring, I do not like to see riding horse types in the hack classes, particularly in the large classes. Nor do I like to see exhibitors circling the judge rather than using the full ring and, likewise,

Fig 117 *Donald Owen riding Sporting Rights (Middle-weight Hunter of the Year 1968) after winning the Hunter Championship at the Bath and West Show.*

judges following a certain horse round the ring instead of watching all the competitors on one side. In my opinion individual shows are generally too stereotyped, though to introduce something different like a dressage type movement which is elegant and not mechanical into a hack class is very difficult and, of course, one is never sure of the reaction of the judge. It is safer to keep individual shows simple and straightforward, showing obedience to hand and leg. Changes of pace must be flowing and pleasing to the eye, retaining elegance, which is sometimes lost when the canter becomes too strong. The trot should be slow and elegant with the horse landing on his toe, not his heel (which happens

when the trot is rushed). It is amazing how many people exaggerate a horse's failing at this pace by rushing, in the hope of forcing a stride which is not there.

I am worried that horses are artificially set up in front which results in animals going hollow-backed and in two halves – the bridge collapses and the horse cannot carry the load. It is the forehand that becomes elevated with correct schooling, not the neck.

Over the years, the showing world has changed. The true professional showmen who commanded one's respect and who would give a few words of free advice with no thought of gain (which would often result in tremendous improvement) have almost gone. The enthusiasm and

*Fig 118   John Keen on Formidable, Hack of the Year 1988
(and large Hack of the Year 1989) which the late Count Robert
Orssich described as 'a swan on a lake' when moving.*

pleasure derived by these horsemen when they could help (the help being received with gratitude and a result achieved), brought a tremendous warmth which does not seem to be there today. I am concerned that in this day of increasing costs, unless shows are encouraged to stage showing classes, these will be the first to go, which will be the end of showing as we know it.

Occasionally, I am asked if there are any particular incidents that have amused me during my years in showing. I immediately recall one occasion at a spring show of which I am a committee member. One of the hunter judges sud-denly became extremely ill, but he con-tinued judging until finally, he had to take one of the exhibits quietly back to the rider and groom (who was also the owner) saying, 'Sorry, please excuse me'. He reappeared a few minutes later say, 'I am sorry – I had to be sick'. The owner turned to the rider and said 'I knew you had ruined this horse's ride – it's even making the judges ill now!'

In conclusion, I think that the best advice would be to watch everything and learn – eventing, dressage, show-jump-ing – in fact, any horse activity, after all it is free! By doing this, you can even learn from other people's mistakes. Watch a particular favourite who has perfected his craft and whose style and technique you admire. I remember the late Jack Gittins telling me that riding a young horse around a show ground can do more to educate him than anything at home. This was when I gave his young horse a lead around a busy show field in and out of the sheep pens on my small hunter for a couple of hours. The horse, even though he was still green, won a major Championship the day after!

Hunters by Vin Toulson

Vin Toulson, who comes from a Lincolnshire farming family, was very much involved in National Hunt racing as an amateur rider before showing. In fact, it was through riding Pan Handle (on whom he won seven handicap chases on the trot) that he met his wife Daphne, who actually owned the horse.

Together with their head girl of twenty-five years, Jean Andrews, they have produced such notable hunter champions as Princes Street, Elite, Dual Gold, Seabrook, Sporting Print and Assurance for such notable owners as the South Essex Insurance Group and the Countess of Inchcape, amongst others, and Lady Zinnia Judd, who was 'a very knowledgeable owner and never asked for explanations if things went wrong'.

However, two of his favourite moments were when he qualified Seabrook for Wembley in the working hunter class at Moreton in 1989 and one year at the Royal Show (which is his favourite show), when he won both the four-year-old and the novice classes on two different horses.

Vin's first big success was leading the winning lead rein pony Mainoaks Delight at Royal Windsor (with his niece on board), which he had bought for very little money at Harry Llewellyn's sale. It took him fifteen years to get to the top of the show hunter ladder, as most of the horses he could afford to buy before then often had problems. In 1973, he produced Sporting Print (Small Hunter of the Year), and his first Open Wembley Champion, the Irish Thoroughbred heavyweight Princes Street, (by the renowned sire Black Tarquin) who had only finished racing in March of that year (then called Passing Light). It said much for Vin's horsemanship that he was able to produce a hunter Champion out of a horse that had been racing only three months previously and proves that this can be achieved. Unfortunately, Princes Street was retired from the show ring when a new HIS rule barring hobdayed horses came into force the following year.

I would sooner have a heavyweight horse that is a stone under the weight but with breeding, than one that is up to the weight but common. 'Breeding will carry a heavy man better out hunting than a big common brute who will tire easily, simply by the way he goes.'

I like to show horses that have been in training as they know how to go forward and have usually been educated. Once a

Fig 119   Vin Toulson on the Thoroughbred Heavyweight, Princes Street, Show Hunter of the Year 1973, pictured here in the collecting ring at the Royal Show after winning the Hunter Championship.

show hunter is schooled, there is no need to overwork him, running the risk of boring the animal and turning him sour. All my show horses go out in the field when they return from a show to have a roll – this also keeps them sober. I believe that 70 per cent of the show hunter's success is based on manners; after all, what is the point of having a good-looking horse if no one can ride him?

When judging or buying a horse, I can forgive a few things if he is a good mover and a good galloper. I particularly remember an extremely good galloper that I showed to win a major Championship, after he had galloped out of the ring

and back in through the other entrance, without the judge noticing! However, I am very concerned that a lot of people on the hunter judging panel will often choose something that gallops fast, at the expense of good conformation and, worse still, soundness. I should like to see more horses being asked to change the rein and gallop on the left rein as a class (just as you would do out hunting) and one of my pet hates is when horses enter the ring at a trot instead of at a walk.

Over the years, the horses have become too big and we have lost our genuine 12st 7lbs ladies' horses like Monbra who won the Horse of the Year hunter title in 1966 and Patricia Cope's

Mighty Grand, the 1955/56 Horse of the Year Champion.

I also believe that there is too much money in present-day showing, which often attracts a lot of new owners who do not understand horses and just want the publicity instead. We are losing the true horse owner because the costs of showing are continually rising. There are two things that I think would keep and encourage more exhibitors into the game. Firstly, stabling should be given free or should be heavily subsidized at the large shows that make a lot of money at the gate, or at least refunded if they are not used. Secondly, some substitution system should be adopted, possibly along the lines of the BSJA, so that if your horse goes lame, at least the entry can be used, (possibly by a new horse who was not ready at the closing date of entries and therefore not entered). I should also like to see more classes for the novice rider who probably does not have a top-class horse, so that everyone is catered for – all for the good of showing.

Cobs by Robert Oliver

Robert Oliver is considered by many to be the top showman of modern-day showing. Apart from his innumerable successes in the show ring with hacks and hunters, he has to date won the Cob of the Year title six times with Cromwell, Kempley and more recently with Super Ted.

The cob, as the saying goes, should have 'the head of a lady and the backside of a cook'. A quality head, well set on, a shoulder that is not too straight, together with a short back and deep girth are all points to look for, as well as short cannon bones with plenty of bone and good clean hocks.

The show cob should be a show heavyweight hunter in miniature. The animal that is common, both in looks and movement, and more suited to a cart should always be avoided. Many cobs pull and go on their forehand, and so are unpleasant to ride, which can be avoided if their schooling is not rushed. Time must be spent teaching the correct aids and making them supple, so that they can work with their hind legs underneath them to lighten the forehand. When this is achieved the cob can be a very enjoyable ride. Many exhibitors and judges tend to over-gallop cobs, thus making them sharper and more excitable in the ring.

Many cobs are shown far too fat and unfit with great cresty necks. Not only does this put undue strain on limbs and wind but also looks unsightly. A good covering of flesh is all that is required, thus helping to keep the cobs' quality. Quality is extremely difficult to define and only by experience can you hope to recognize a truly quality cob. The best ones should be capable of carrying any member of the family with hounds all day.

The height of cobs has been the subject of lengthy discussion in the past year or two. Many people think that the present limit of 15.1hh should be raised to

15.2hh, one inch over the height permitted by the British Show Hack, Cob & Riding Horse Association. In my opinion, this would allow cobs of hunter type to be shown. Since these will often give a freer, sharper ride, it means that the steadiness, manners, and the correct type of show cob would gradually be lost. Cobs rarely have a defined wither. Many are low loaded in the shoulder; therefore they often give the impression of being higher than they actually are.

Interest in the show cob is such that the good cob is hard to find both in England and Ireland. Prices now range from £5,000 – £10,000. However, care must be taken when purchasing a young cob, especially Irish bred ones because their unknown breeding means that they tend to grow until they are six or seven years old. Those with pony blood are, of course, more likely to stay within the height limit.

Fig 120   Robert Oliver at home with Kempley, Cob of the Year 1977, 1978 and 1979.

Working Hunter and Show Hunter Ponies by Sandra Bucknell

Sandra Bucknell is one of the most respected and sought after WHP/SHP judges on the circuit today. Ponies she has produced include Simple Simon (13hh) who was Nursery Stakes champion at the BSPS Championship Show in 1974, Tonto (14hh) who was reserve Working Hunter Pony of the Year in 1976 (having previously been Champion Working Hunter Pony of the Year in 1970 and 1971 with owner Tiny Clapham who is now extremely successful in the eventing world) and Pageboy (15hh) who was many times a Champion.

When I am judging at a show, I always pray that my ring will be big enough for my competitors to gallop in and that the course will be built and ready. My dream is to find a lovely solid, flowing course, presented with plenty of fillers and some greenery, so all I have to do is check the stridings in any combinations, fence-related distances and finally check the height and width for my first class. Unfortunately, I frequently arrive to find all sorts of terrible courses, sometimes built, sometimes just lying in heaps on the ground and it is sheer agony trying to build a course on your own, with about six pairs of wings, a dozen poles and one filler, and with endless competitors and their followers all asking 'When will the class start and where are jumps four and five?' The basic problem here is a desperate lack of good course builders. This is a true art and all the societies like the BSPS and the HIS should all do much more to help and encourage people to study and practise the subject; until they put their minds to it fully, judges will continue to arrive at shows to find sub-standard courses and jumps.

I like to see WHPs jump their fences in a good, forward-going and purposeful manner, balanced and rhythmic, with as little adjustment from the rider as possible (except to increase or decrease pace as necessary for combinations or bounces and so on). I have no particular preference for tack. In the children's classes, I am quite happy to accept whatever suits child and pony, but I do often feel very sorry for some children who have to jump on straight-cut show saddles. I know they might show off a pony's shoulder, but having nowhere to put your knees is a horrid feeling and does nothing for a child's position over a fence. If a working pony has a good shoulder, it will easily accommodate a saddle with knee rolls.

My ideal WHP is a stronger type of pony, as I have always believed that working ponies should be able to work; they must have plenty of bone and be active, well-balanced rides. I have always found that correct conformation in a pony generally means that it would be able to do just about everything: hunt all day; do an adequate dressage test; and, as

long as it was courageous, jump either coloured, rustic or cross-country fences, both at speed or at a more balanced WHP pace or in a shorter, more precise show-jumping style. Sadly, I think people today tend to coddle their WHPs far too much. A happy pony is usually one that competes in all sorts of different disciplines.

The Pony Club is an excellent organization for children to compete at all sorts of events, both individually and as team members. All these experiences are invaluable to both pony and rider, especially when they compete at the bigger shows with long cleverly designed courses where judgement of pace and correct approaches become so important. Of course, the ultimate schooling ground is the hunting field; there is nothing to compare with a great day's hunting and it is sad that more children do not get the chance to experience it. The Pony Club is able to help many children with their own Pony Club meets, which most hunts hold in the Christmas holidays. A word of warning here, though. Parents should never send their children hunting without proper supervision.

Perhaps one of the reasons some WHPs are not hunted is the fear of their acquiring scars and blemishes, but if I am judging and I find a scar or blemish on a WHP, it does not bother me too much. I would rather see a blemish acquired from working than see a couple of unsightly splints acquired because of a lack of good bone or poor movement. As regards scars on show hunter ponies, I feel that in the perfect world these should not be acceptable because I try to make a certain distinction between a worker and a show animal, and I do not wish to see scars on my show hunter ponies.

175

My advice to everyone with WHPs is go and do everything with your pony. You will surely enjoy them all the more and gain valuable experience along the way. They are far more likely to keep pleasing you if you give them variety in their work. We had three wonderful working ponies in Simple Simon (13hh), Tonto, (14hh) and Pageboy (15hh). They all hunted hard, were regular Pony Club Team members in all the disciplines and all three retired without any blemishes, scars, windgalls, splints or lameness problems at all, which has to be mainly due to good conformation, straight movement and a little bit of luck, which we all need. So good luck with your workers, enjoy them as we enjoyed ours and give me many more happy days judging you.

Show Ponies by Stella Harries

Stella was in fact named after a pony that won at Olympia and rode many winning ponies including Kavora Mr. Chips who was Champion at Richmond in 1949 and the 14.2hh grey Kavora Dubarry, who was Reserve Champion to Scarlet Knipe (neé Rimmell) on Peter Pan at the RIHS. Stella went to work with the late Count Robert Orssich for eighteen months and feels priviledged to have watched him work his horses at such close quarters where she could appreciate the knowledge he had gained from the Spanish School and old traditional methods.

Over the years she has produced such notable champions as Arden Tittle Tattle, Shandon, Kavora Kind Sir, Touchdown and her particular favourite Pollyanna, 'who would still win today'.

She believes parents should be behind the trainers 100 per cent to instil discipline into the children having had a very strict upbringing herself. When she was ten years old, Stella was offered the ride on Kavora Jet at the RIHS, but her father did not consider her to be ready for such a big occasion. The pony won and was Reserve to Legend, ridden by Felicity Phillips, who was tragically killed the following year in an accident with a lorry whilst out on the road with her pony. (The 12.2hh cup at the RIHS is named after her).

Stella's lessons are often a mixture of hard work and fun, in which she not only instructs her pupils, but also explains the reasons for carrying out certain exercises. Cathryn Cooper who achieved so much success with Holly of Spring, was her favourite pupil as she was dedicated and could take criticism, which was very useful when she made the transition from ponies to horses.

When buying a pony, you cannot alter the basic conformation, but if the framework is correct you can, with production, put muscle in the right place and improve the way of going. A pony that looks good in outline and goes well will be successful (whereas a hack has also to give a very good ride to be a Champion), therefore the pony jockey is of paramount importance, being the person who

Fig 121 Tonto, ridden by Alison Bucknell, Working Hunter Pony of the Year 1970/71.

conveys to the judge that his mount is beautifully schooled, even if he isn't! I particularly enjoy matching talent with talent – a top jockey with a Champion pony.

Ponies are more natural animals and go forward more automatically, and problems arise when teenagers move into horses and find difficulty in keeping them between hand and leg. I believe that juniors should go straight into the adult classes, although I can appreciate the commercial advantages of the intermediate classes. However, I do not like to see good horses being down-graded in intermediate classes, just to win a red rosette.

Sadly, a lot of owners who can afford expensive animals want instant results and are not prepared to wait as the professional owners of old were. As a result, even though the overall standard is higher in today's showing, most of the ponies lack charisma, looking bored and with clockwork movement caused by over-showing and bad production (often in rings that are overcrowded). In the past, ponies were more individual and were presented with a touch of class.

I have fond memories of the wide open spaces and relaxed atmosphere of the class shows like White City and Richmond compared to the tense limitations of the present-day preliminary judging at Wembley. Although Wembley is a wonderful climax to the end of the season, too many people place too much emphasis on this one show (probably because of the

Fig 122 Pollyanna, Show Pony of the Year 1963 (Reserve in 1962), by Bwlch Valentino ex Pretty Polly. This 13.2 hh mare was owned and bred by the late Albert Deptford and produced by Stella Harries. She was sold to America for £8,000 and left England three days before Christmas in 1963.

the same enthusiasm is not shown towards the other major shows during the summer.

In my opinion, dope testing should be more randomly carried out and samples should be taken at smaller shows and on ponies further down the line. It is the people who are least suspected who, in their confidence, could be up to all sorts of tricks.

I also believe that the measuring system should be tightened. If it were, there would be no need for objections. I feel strongly that a height certificate should have more credibility especially as the costs of these are continually rising – like everything else in showing (hence the increase of company sponsorship).

Finally, I feel that the high standard of judging must be maintained. I am frequently amazed at some people's overconfidence in attending the assessments in the first place, when they have probably only produced one or possibly two made ponies.

trouble they have had to go to in order to qualify for it) and it is a pity that

Ridden Mountain and Moorland Ponies by Sally Coles

Sally Coles is very much involved in the production of in hand and ridden Mountain and Moorland ponies, and owns the successful Connemara Ballydonagh Misterina who was three-times Champion in hand at the Royal, third in the Lloyds Bank final and qualified for Olympia three years running (being best of breed one year). She also rode Glansevin Gay Gordon, Chiltern Demelza, Gaylesbrook Kiera and produced Paddock Gemini under saddle.

In recent years, the true worth of the native ponies of the British Isles has finally been realized on a large scale. Faced with prices – real or rumoured – well beyond their pockets for show ponies, families have sought and found an alternative in the native breeds, which now have an increasing range of classes to compete in, with adult riders permitted.

With the introduction of lead-rein and

first ridden Mountain and Moorland classes, more use can be made of the smaller breeds and should result in fuller use being made of their versatility.

If you are looking for success in the classes that qualify for the major Championships – Olympia, Malvern, Ponies UK and so on – it is of prime importance that the animal you are exhibiting is easily recognizable for the breed that it is. Any doubt in the judge's mind (is that pony a small Section B, or is it a Section A or even a Dartmoor?) will not help you to stand at the top of the line.

Having decided that the Mountain and Moorland section is the one you want to compete in, and you have a specific breed in mind, a trip to the relevant breed show is a worthwhile experience. You will be able to see the different types within a breed and compare them together. Notice what the judges (who are experts on their particular breed) place particular emphasis on for that breed: make and shape, feet, action which are the essential characteristics of recognizable type.

When choosing a pony, pay particular attention to the length of stride in walk. If the basic conformation is such that the strides are short and restricted, there is not a great deal you can do to make the strides very much longer. It is in this pace that the judge first sees you, and from which they usually make their final selection. Whatever specific criteria are applied to the action in trot for each breed, the hind legs should be active, with strides of good length – not necessarily flashy or of the toe-pointing variety.

Although the weight-carrying ability of the small breeds is well known, to present the best possible overall impression in a ridden class, it is preferable for the pony and rider to be in proportion.

Fig 123   Sally Coles on her Champion Connemara Ballydonagh Misterina at Olympia, who also finished third in the Lloyds In Hand final in 1987.

While some of the breeds come from origins where riding was not their main use in life and their conformation does not always lend itself ideally to being ridden as much as some of the other riding type breeds, with careful schooling the 'heavies' can give impressive shows conveying power and strength.

It is important to assess the pony's way of going. A pony should never give the impression of being propped up by the rider's hands, with the front legs pulling the body instead of the hind legs carrying the body and propelling it along. The overall impression should be of obedience, balance and suppleness and the rider can do much to cover up any flaws in the way of going by having a steady position, independent of the reins.

179

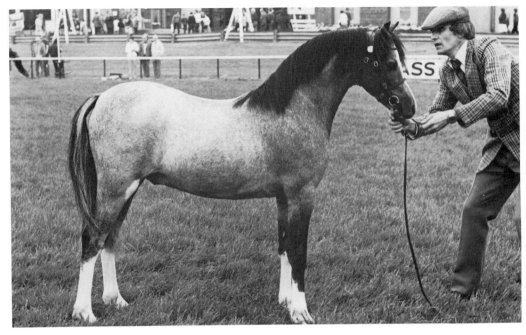

Fig 124   David Blair with Welsh Section A Champion Waxwing Herod, who qualified for the Lloyds as a yearling at the Royal (the youngest ever native pony to date to qualify). He was exported to Australia the next year after covering a selected number of mares.

All the breed societies have their own rules regarding trimming – some more explicit than others – and it is most important that you are sure of the variations of interpretation before even picking up your scissors, combs and clippers. If clipping for the early indoor shows, or for Olympia (if you are fortunate enough to qualify), a point worth bearing in mind is that a full clip as opposed to a hunter clip can leave the lower legs looking distinctly bare and light of bone.

For those ponies who also take part in BSPS SHP/WHP classes, where plaiting is the norm, it is not possible to have an untrimmed mane, but do try to leave it a little longer to avoid the scalped look when in the Mountain and Moorland section. Resist the temptation to go for too much of a show pony look: brightly coloured browbands, ties and buttonholes distract the eye from the individuality of the native breeds. With the wide variety of tweed jackets that are available, it is still possible to avoid getting lost in a large class, and black or dark navy does suit some colours of native pony.

As with any show animal, your choice of tack must complement your pony's features: stitched, narrow bridles do nothing for many native heads, broader nose and brow bands can be much more flattering. Be prepared to spend some considerable time searching for the right saddle. Broad-barrelled ponies with only a suggestion of a wither are notoriously difficult to fit with a saddle. The minute show-pony type of saddle without a full panel but with ultra straight flaps and flat seat does not suit many natives. Nor does it stay in the right place to assist the rider to look elegant.

With the advent of the NPS novice ridden Mountain and Moorland Championship, perhaps now is the time to start looking for your native pony of the future.

Ridden Mountain and Moorland Champions at Olympia

1978	Criffell Casper	Welsh Section B
1979	Senruf Grebe	Dartmoor
1980	Rosenharley Laurin	Connemara
1981	Norwood Principal Boy	Welsh Section B
1982	Grayswood Village Peregrine	Connemara
1983 / 1984	Rosenharley Rossleague	Connemara
1985	Phineas Phinn	Connemara
1986	Wiston Llwynog	Welsh Section D
1987	Dunrowan Dolphin	Highland
1988	Marston Monsoon	Welsh Section B
1989	Persie Ramrod	Welsh Section C

Arabs by Valerie Mallender

The Mallender name is well known and highly respected in the Arab world. Famous names to be produced from the Mallender stable include; Micawber (fourth in the Fredericks final in 1967), My Colleen, Starlight Serenade, Grand Surprise, Prince Amlah and Merry Michael to name but a few and all achieved enormous success both in hand and under saddle not only in the show ring but also in a wide variety of equestrian spheres.

My first introduction to Arab horses came when I stayed with Henry and Julia Wynmalen in 1942 and I was inspired with great enthusiasm after meeting their famous stallion Basa, his part-bred Arab son Bascar and the rest of their beautiful horses. Henry then enrolled me as a member of the Arab Horse Society.

The Arabian is one of the oldest breeds known, going back many centuries. Everyone, I am sure, knows that the present day Thoroughbred is descended from three Arabian stallions: Byerley Turk, imported in 1689; the Darley Arabian in 1705; and the Godolphin Arabian in 1728. Many other breeds have had infusions of Arab blood to improve and upgrade them.

Wilfred Scawen Blunt and his wife Lady Ann Blunt (the mother of Lady Wentworth) brought many fine Arabians to this country to found their large stud. Apart from this stud, there were some small studs and a few Arabs owned

181

by a handful of people, mainly officers who had brought their chargers home from the East. Obviously, there were no shows for them in the early days but in 1864, a class for 'Eastern Bred Horses' was held in London. An entry of three Barb and six Arabs was the total forward and the prize money was £20. Early in the twentieth century, classes for Arab stallions were held in the shows at Islington run by the National Pony Society, which was founded in 1893. These classes were for Arabs as polo pony sires; unfortunately the entries were very small, the stallions themselves being around 14.2hh.

The Arab Horse Society was founded in 1918 by Mr Musgrave Clark and the Rev. D. B. Montiefore (who was President of the NPS in 1903). It was formed to encourage, among other things, the use of Arab blood in light horse breeding and so through the years the number of pure-Anglo, and part-bred Arabs grew to the number they are today, with show classes increasing to match.

Anglo Arabs have no other blood than pure Arab and Thoroughbred in their pedigree and a part-bred must have not less than 25 per cent Arab blood. In the early days, there was a pure-bred Arab section in the General Stud Book. This was brought to an end in 1965, but Anglo-Arab stallions and mares already registered in the stud book remained and when any of these horses were mated with a Thoroughbred, the progeny was and still is eligible for registration. There are at least three listed Anglo-Arab stallions in the General Stud Book who could quite legitimately sire a classic winner, although this is probably most unlikely.

The Arab has a wonderful character: very kind, intelligent, courageous, very anxious to please and quick to learn; and since they are very comfortable to ride, they make very good ridden horses.

Naseel, the Arab pony stallion owned by Mrs Nicholson, has left a great mark on ponies. Having sired such ponies as Pretty Polly, My Pretty Maid and others, the bloodlines have been handed down and are still to the fore in today's show ponies. Naseel was a very versatile stallion, siring show hacks, hunters and cobs. In 1956, I bought a yearling Arab gelding Sahla who grew to 15.1hh. When he was broken, I wished to show him under saddle (1959/60) but found that there were virtually no ridden Arab classes for him. So I plaited him up and showed him very successfully, up to County level, in show hack and small hunter classes and he always gave the judges a good ride. Later, I hunted him a season with the Meynell and no day was too long nor jump too high for him and he hacked to and from the meet each time.

The trend today is to breed the bigger type of animal – in all three sections of Arab breeding. No doubt it makes them more useful for racing, eventing and so on, but I feel that some of the quality is lost on the way. I like my Anglo Arabs to have between 50 and 75 per cent Arab blood and, surprisingly, very few I think have looked too 'Araby' in competition with other animals.

I believe that as a young horse moves naturally and freely in the field, so one should try to reproduce this as nearly as possible in the show ring. So many of the Arabs (in all sections) are asked to trot far faster than their natural movement allows, causing their hocks to trail and go wide behind, which gives the impression of weakness. After all, good hocks are

Fig 125 Forge Gay Galliard, ridden by Rebecca Mitchell, a big winner of part-bred Arab ridden (and small hack) classes. Twice Champion at the Northern Arab Show and three times Champion at the East of England.

Fig 126 Desert Storm, by the French Anglo-Arab stallion Connetable, collecting the Horse and Hound Cup from the Editor Mr W. O. Case, after winning the Hack of the Year title in 1961 (a repeat of 1959).

essential to the riding horse as they are required to give strength and impulsion and enable the horse to move freely from the shoulder.

The new American fashion is fast taking hold in the shows in Britain and I am not sure how the youngster, who is taught to have an unnaturally high head carriage (which must affect the spine and therefore the hocks), is going to readjust

to become a riding horse of totally different shape. The true line of the Arabian horse is very beautiful and the subject of many paintings and drawings.

In ridden classes in the show ring, the pure-, Anglo- and part-bred Arabs have to be very versatile. They are required to be well schooled with the manners and ride of the show hack and the ability to gallop like a hunter.

In Hand Showing by Tom Best and David Blair

Partners in the famous Waxwing stud, their high standard of production of in hand ponies is renowned and dedication much admired. They have twice qualified Paddock Gemini for the Lloyds at the Royal Highland Show, considered to be their local show, as well as qualifying the yearling Waxwing Herod at the Royal Show. Since then he has been exported to Australia where he has been the leading sire for the last three years.

From years of experience of either producing ponies or watching others who do, we firmly believe that there are only a few principles that are outstanding in the art of show ring practice.

Firstly, assuming that many people can get animals to look well, there is the art of getting animals to go well. There is no question that performance has much greater status in the ridden classes, which is possibly why in hand producers place less emphasis on that part of their own production. However, good performances are not only expected of our own in hand animals, but hold the balance of power when there is not much to choose between exhibits.

Very few exhibitors can achieve consistency of performance in their animals which is why those who can are outstanding in their production technique. Their approaches may differ but one thing that is common to them all, is that they have a firm grasp of ridden performance as well. The still head, the active hock and the balanced, forward action is commonplace in all categories of showing.

Unfortunately, there is an alarming trend towards the use of side reins, running reins, martingales and whatever else to produce a contrived manner of going. Used correctly, these devices can have meaningful effects. Sadly, we witness the side-effects of misuse: the over-bending, the stiff board-like immobility and the shortening of stride. In young ponies in particular, the zombie-like product is far removed from that of nature. Believe it or not, within the artificial confines of the show ring, it is still possible to produce a nearly natural product.

Secondly, there is the attention to detail – something that we believe is of paramount importance when it comes to the higher levels of showing. This covers a wide span of criteria, ranging from buckles on bridles, to mane and tail lengths. The secret of this fine tuning comes from years of watching, observing, adapting then adopting, but only when appropriate – that is the key. Details are never obtrusive; they are always discreet. In total, they complete the picture. Invariably, they are noticeable by their absence.

Lastly, and possibly most difficult to achieve, is that unquantifiable quality of self-criticism. How many of us can, or are prepared to, stand back and analyse our performance in a critical way? How often do we compare our own product with that of others? How often have we blamed the judge, when we should have been blaming ourselves? We never escape from the learning process; to wish to would be folly. In order to do well, and moreover to continue to do well as producers, we have no choice but to continue to ask questions. Without doubt, these questions begin with ourselves in an honest and frank analysis of our own performance. By facing up to this difficult task, we are in a position from which we are able to progress.

All three of the principles tackled in this short statement are complementary. They are all part of the visual image which the exhibitor attempts to produce. By tackling the issues outside the ring, in our view, it is more likely that victories will be won within it.

The Riding Horse by Richard Ramsay

Richard Ramsay is very much a specialist at finding and producing riding horses of the right type. First Glance (three times Champion at Royal Windsor) and Sound of Music (twice winner at the RIHS) were two of my particular favourites which came from the Ramsay yard. Richard also produced and rode Meridian to win the Riding Horse of the Year title at Wembley when the classes returned in 1986.

Ten years ago, the riding horse class was the poor relation of the showing world, with classes to be found at the smaller shows and generally reckoned to cater for the misfit horse, though they were frequently used by hack and hunter exhibitors as a school for their horses. But the British Show Hack and Cob Association, mainly thanks to the efforts of Mrs Dorian Williams, began to realize that with the scarcity of the true hack and the increasing size and weight of the hunters, there was a huge gap in the show world for a horse that no longer appeared to have a suitable class. Thus the official small and large riding horse classes were given proper recognition and incorporated into The British Show Hack & Cob Association so that they could be defined and shown under proper rules.

These classes were an immediate success. The Association managed to get a Championship class at Bucks County Show and then with the birth of the Hack, Cob and Riding Horse Association National Championship Show, they had their supreme Championship there. With the increasing interest and support for the classes, and the high standard of animals coming forward, some of the bigger shows began to take notice. The Royal International introduced the classes into its schedule and then the riding horse finally achieved total recognition by being given classes at the Horse of the Year Show.

Already, some of the past and present Champions have been recognized as outstanding horses. In the smalls, First Glance, Sound of Music, Panache, JCB and Fair Breeze immediately come to mind; and in the larger category, Burroprince, Preview, Appollo and Brown Sabre could hold their own anywhere.

Many people ask what a riding horse is and gradually a type has emerged. The small riding horse should be a quality animal with correct conformation and

185

Fig 127   Richard Ramsay returning to the line-up after his individual show in the Riding Horse Championship (which he won) at Wembley in 1986 with large-class winner Meridian. Judges Judy Bradwell and Nat Sherwood look on.

good limbs, without needing to have quite the substance of the true small hunter or quite the refinement of the true hack. The large riding horse should be a larger version of the former, in many cases the sort of horse one would see in a Munnings picture, a lovely type of blood horse ideally about 16.1hh. In all cases, the movement should be straight and free and, as in other show classes, the horse should be devoid of blemishes and serious faults, such as curbs. The riding horse should be a very educated ride, as the accent is very much on the ride. What the judge should look for are three correct paces, the ability to lengthen into a gallop and, of course, good manners (which are of paramount importance). One need not expect the riding horse to have the ex-

Fig 128   First Glance, a good type of small riding horse on his way to winning the Championship at Royal Windsor Horse Show. Well presented by Lulu McAlpine and produced by Richard Ramsay.

186

treme lightness in hand of the true hack, but he should not be heavy or strong in his ride either; in other words, he must have self-carriage and be totally even on both reins. He should take the rider freely forward and be responsive to the aids without being sharp. One could easily visualize the riding horse ably perform-ing a good dressage test one day, and carrying his owner across country for a rural ride the next, as well as having the quality and conformation to shine in the show ring.

In conclusion, the riding horse is a beautifully educated all-rounder that is a great pleasure to own.

Riding Side-Saddle by Ronnie Marmont

Ronnie Marmont's magical production of ladies' hunters was considered to be streets ahead of anyone else's. His first big winner, and probably the best, was Rajah who won at the RIHS no less than four times, closely followed by Cufflink, Bright and Breezy and South Pacific who was purchased from the Duke of Westminster at a weekend party in Cheshire and was ridden with great understanding by Joan Gibson as he could be very tricky at times.

Side-saddle riding, which has seen a revival since 1970, creates a most beautiful picture when performed and presented properly, but unless it is approached professionally and executed well, it can become a travesty and an embarrassment to all.

It is imperative that you find the right sort of saddle, for without it, you may as well ride astride. Rather than buy a new saddle, which can be very expensive and most of the time not ideal, I would advise advertising for a good quality second-hand one, preferably by Mayhew, Champion and Wilton, or Owen (these are my favourites) which can vary in price depending on the condition. Preferably, buy one with a stirrup and leather other-wise you could have problems finding one to match the fitting, particularly with some of the old ones. Also, many well-used saddles will need restuffing by an expert to suit your horse, which does not come cheap. The seat must be absolutely level and the pommels must be wide apart so that you can sit relaxed with your left leg as an astride leg. At all costs, avoid the dip-seated saddles that make the riders feel as though they are riding downhill and look as if they are sitting in a hip bath.

I have seen so many young ladies sitting on the most dreadful large saddles which cover almost all of the horse and on enquiry, have discovered that they had leased them for the show season from someone who assured them that they were perfect for the job. Avoid this situation by taking with you an expert who really knows what you want.

The balance strap should be gradually fastened not too tightly nor too far back, otherwise this could lead to bucking. Nor should it be too slack, otherwise unneces-sary movement will give the horse a sore back. It should be just enough to hold the back of the saddle in place.

The turn-out in a side-saddle class simply must be smart and correct. Do not

187

Fig 129   Cufflink, the naughty four-year old – ridden here by Mrs Bea Haggas – became one of the best ladies' horses and was a dream ride in a side-saddle. The saddle shown here is a Mayhew. Note the girth strap is on the outside, which is very smart. The habit is by Roberts and Carroll.

Fig 130   Midnight Sun, Small Hack of the Year 1967 and a prolific winner of ladies' classes, pictured here winning at Royal Windsor with Jane Bullen on board.

overdress. Again, the second-hand market is your best bet. I have seen many modern ready-mades on tack stands at shows – but they are not for me. If you advertise you may be luck enough to obtain a Roberts and Carroll or Busvine habit and if you can get one that fits perfectly you will be very lucky. There are still some about that have been treasured for years or have been outgrown. If you can afford to have a new one made, go straight to Bernard Weatherall – the cost will be high but they are the best. Otherwise Frank Hall of Market Harborough's account might be somewhat less frightening and they are also very good. To either of these tailors you should take your own

side-saddle for fittings, as the apron must hang properly and sadly, the side-saddles in tailors' fitting rooms are of the hip-bath variety. I like to see children in side-saddle classes in blue habits in not too heavy a cloth, although some of the tweed habits can be very smart. Always wear a collar and neat tie. Matching breeches and beautifully polished boots perfect the outfit even though they are hidden by your apron. The younger girls must wear a hunting cap but when they are older a small neat bowler is smart with the hair done in the correct way (a bun and hairnet), and I like to see a veil. The golden rule for adults is to wear a bowler hat with a veil before noon and a top hat, veil and white hunting tie in the afternoon.

Most well-balanced astride horses and ponies will readily take to this form of riding once accustomed to the side-

*Fig 131   Fidelio, Working Hunter of the Year 1975, equally
successful in lightweight and ladies' hunter classes.*

saddle, which must not be too heavy.
The horses most suitable are not necessarily the flashy extravagant movers, in
fact they often detract considerably from
the ring performance as a smooth, collected and well-balanced trot is what most
judges are looking for, apart from the fact
that there is nothing more bone shaking
than an extended trot when riding side-
saddle.

An assistant on the ground will be
invaluable in teaching you to sit up
straight and in the middle, keeping your
right shoulder back, which at times is
difficult to feel when on board. As
astride, if your leg position comes back,
you will be tipped forward and vice

versa, apart from the fact you will lose the
grip which keeps you secure in the side-
saddle. Similarly, if you lean to either
side, it may make your horse go crooked
as well as run the risk of bringing him
down at faster paces. The most common
fault is when the jockey leans to the right
to compensate for the lack of leg support
that you have when riding astride.

If the rider is insecure in the seat and
round shouldered owing to tension, this
looks worse when riding side-saddle than
when riding astride. Apart from the
appearance of it, bouncing around will
eventually give the horse a sore back.
When riding side-saddle, the picture
should above all be one of elegance.

10 Reflections

My first recollection of a showing class is when I visited the Royal Lancashire Show at Blackpool as a child and watched a class of 12.2hh show ponies. If my memory serves me right, it was like looking into another world. Even though I was spellbound at the time, I could never have imagined that some years later I would be totally involved in this world of showing and that at an even later date I would actually be writing a book on the subject! In showing, it is a fact that you never know what is waiting for you around the corner and that you must be prepared for the ups and the downs of the sport.

Over the years I have enjoyed training a great number of animals ranging from Arabs to heavyweight hunters. Some have disappointed, others have lived up to more than expectations. Perhaps the most exciting of these ventures has been taking novices to the top, which is much more enjoyable than keeping a Champion there. The ultimate thrill however, is to produce that special moment which delights both the scientific and artistic spectator: when the animal's performance is magic – technically and visually. More importantly I have met many kind people from all walks of life, some of whom have become lifelong friends and it is to these people that I have dedicated this book.

In my opinion, it is the responsibility of those in charge to make sure that the sport moves in the right direction and that sportsmanship is safeguarded in this commercial age. I am optimistic that this will happen as many exhibitors (both young and old) and breeders with a vast wealth of knowledge and experience behind them often become judges, council members and show organizers, proving that showing is a continuous process and can look forward to a rosy future.

Finally, I should like to wish you the very best of luck, something we all need at times, and many happy moments in the show ring.

Index